COINTELPRO

THE FBI's SECRET WAR ON POLITICAL FREEDOM

BY NELSON BLACKSTOCK WITH AN INTRODUCTION BY NOAM CHOMSKY

VINTAGE BOOKS
A DIVISION OF RANDOM HOUSE
NEW YORK

FIRST VINTAGE BOOKS EDITION, July 1976

This book includes, in revised form, material from the following issues of the *Militant*: March 28, April 4, April 11, April 18, April 25, May 9, May 16, May 30, June 13, July 4, July 11, and August 8, 1975. This material is used by permission of the *Militant*, 14 Charles Lane, New York, N.Y. 10014.

The first edition of this book was published with the assistance of the Louis M. Rabinowitz Foundation, Inc.

Library of Congress Cataloging in Publication Data

Perkus, Cathy.
Cointelpro: the FBI's secret war on political freedom.

Includes bibliographical references.
1. United States. Federal Bureau of Investigation.
2. Political rights—United States.   3. Civil rights—United States.   I. Title.
HV8141.P37 1976   364.1'32'0973   76-10583
ISBN 0-394-72186-1

Manufactured in the United States of America

Note

The FBI documents reprinted in this book appear exactly as they came out of government files (only smaller). Some of them are a little hard to read, but for the sake of authenticity, none has been retouched. All the censoring, the blotches, handwritten notes, signatures and underlining were done by FBI officials before they turned over the files. Most of the files were forced out by suits against the government; a few became public as a result of the investigation by the Senate Select Committee on Intelligence.

Copies of all the Cointelpro files that have been made public, and information about the suit by the Socialist Workers party and the Young Socialist Alliance against government harassment, are available from the Political Rights Defense Fund, Box 649 Cooper Station, New York, N.Y. 10003. Telephone (212) 691-3270.

The files concerning Muhammad Kenyatta are also available from the American Civil Liberties Union, 22 East 40th Street, New York, N.Y. 10016. Telephone (212) 725-1222.

The files concerning the Black Panther party are also available from the December 4 Committee, 53 West Jackson, Chicago, Ill. 60605. Telephone (312) 341-9766.

Preface

"CO-INTEL-PRO" is FBI lingo for its illegal (and once top-secret) Counterintelligence Program. Cointelpro was part of the FBI's unjustifiable disruption of legal political activities of American citizens—activities protected by the Bill of Rights.

The full story of the FBI's operations is slowly coming out. In the process, proof accumulates that harassment of political activists continues today—despite assurances by top government officials that the program known as Cointelpro was ended formally in April 1971.

What kind of people and organizations become targets of the FBI? What do they stand for? How does FBI harassment affect them, and how are they fighting back?

Some of the answers are told best in the FBI's own words— in files written in language never intended for the eyes of the American people. These files prove that the bureau is a *political* agency. It targets people who have ideas it doesn't like—Black activists, antiwar leaders, socialists, and others. In one well-established case, the House Select Committee on Intelligence found that the FBI has kept a "legitimate American political party" (the Socialist Workers party) under "intensive investigation" for over thirty years without finding evidence for a single federal indictment against the party or any of its members. (During the wartime hysteria of 1941, the FBI did succeed in getting eighteen leaders of the SWP convicted of "conspiracy" and "advocating overthrow of the government." The law the FBI used, the Smith Act, later was declared unconstitutional by the Supreme Court—but not before the eighteen and others went to jail.) The Cointelpro papers detail years of (unsuccess-

vii

ful) FBI efforts to drive that party out of existence and to keep the public from considering a socialist alternative to the Democrats and Republicans.

The chapters that follow are case studies of Cointelpro in action. Because the FBI's attacks are politically motivated, some discussion of the ideas and activities of its victims is important in order to understand Cointelpro. The documents come straight from the bureau's files. These are only examples; they represent FBI harassment of an untold number more people whose files are still secret. (There are known to be over 20,000 pages of Cointelpro files. Only some 1,600 have been made public.)

It is crucial that the American people learn the full truth about the FBI's violations of constitutional rights. Wide public knowledge about these abuses, and public opposition to them, are the best protection we have against the power of the FBI and other agencies.

Many readers will agree with the political ideas of those persecuted by the FBI. Many won't. But we don't have to agree with people's ideas to see the need for defending their right to express themselves freely, without fear of FBI disruption.

Defending the political rights of others protects your own right to hear and evaluate all points of view. That is why it is important to remember what Voltaire said—"I disapprove of what you say, but I will defend to the death your right to say it." Or what the pioneers of the American labor movement said —"An injury to one is an injury to all."

Some recent events show that the surest way to lose your rights is to ignore attacks on the rights of others. Many leading Democrats in government looked the other way during the persecution of Martin Luther King, the disruption of antiwar activities, and the "conspiracy" trials. Those Democrats did as much to lay the basis for the Watergate break-in as did the warped political values of Richard Nixon.

The notion that some ideas are "subversive" is dangerous for anyone who disagrees with an administration in power, or who may in the future. If the tag "subversive," and the harassment that follows, can be applied to some ideas today, they will be applied to *other* ideas tomorrow—that's been proven by many months of revelations of FBI abuses.

It is dangerous to grant the FBI authority, even limited authority, to "investigate" or maintain surveillance of any political group. It is worth noting that the bureau began its now well-documented vendetta against Dr. Martin Luther King by saying it had to keep an eye on him because he "is closely associated with [censored], a member of the Communist party."

It's hard to imagine a greater threat to our constitutional rights than the intervention of police agencies—in any way—in political life.

We are continually learning about the FBI's operations as more of its files become public. (This edition of COINTELPRO, for example, includes some information not available in an earlier one.) More of the story of Cointelpro is out. And more will come out, if public pressure continues. The FBI is not a willing source of information about any of its clandestine operations, especially the disruption program it waged in secret for at least fifteen years. One of the few ways to pry out documents is to sue the government. And even then the bureau heavily censors the documents before they are released.

The first disclosures of some important Cointelpro files came from a Freedom of Information Act suit by NBC reporter Carl Stern. The files he got, in December 1973 and March 1974, were those initiating some of the Cointelpro operations. (Noam Chomsky talks about them and others in the introduction that follows.)

Most of what is now known about the day-to-day disruption tactics of Cointelpro has been made public as a result of a landmark civil liberties suit by the Socialist Workers party and the Young Socialist Alliance. An order by federal judge Thomas P. Griesa in their suit has already forced the FBI to turn over more than a thousand pages of Cointelpro files.

On March 29, 1976, the socialists' suit was responsible for another revelation of the FBI's massive intrusion into the constitutional rights of American citizens. The suit forced the FBI to release documents that prove specially trained teams of agents routinely burglarized the offices of the SWP at least 94 times from 1960 to 1966—*an average of once every three weeks for six and a half years.* Agents stole and photographed documents and correspondence about virtually every aspect of the party's business, including names of campaign contributors and defense strategy of members involved in Federal legal cases. The bureau then used the stolen information to fuel its Cointelpro disruption operations.

As startling as those revelations are, the disclosures also catch the government in an outright lie. The new information about the burglaries and about their use as a routine tactic directly contradicts an official Justice Department assertion in court that the SWP was never a target of government burglaries.

The socialists' suit aims to help expose and curb attacks by the FBI and other police agencies on constitutional rights. It seeks $27 million in damages and a permanent injunction outlawing harassment of all those who disagree with official policy.

Constitutional attorneys Leonard Boudin and Herbert Jordan took the case to court July 18, 1973. At this writing, the suit is still in the "pretrial discovery" stage, forcing more disclosures of government files. It is expected to go to trial in the next year

At the trial the victims of Cointelpro will for the first time be putting the secret agents and their superiors on the witness stand. For a change, it will be the government, and not its targets, on trial. (It is worth noting that the Justice Department has yet to announce any plans to prosecute the conspirators responsible for Cointelpro.)

A court injunction against political spying and harassment will be a historic victory for the rights of everyone. The winners will be the Black movement, trade unions, women's organizations, student groups, socialists, and many others—everyone who has a stake in defending the freedom to engage in political activity without government interference.

The SWP suit has already shown some important results. The case has been part of the public debate about the future of the intelligence agencies. It has encouraged other victims of government harassment to fight back by filing suits and taking other actions to protect their rights. And it has made available to the American people information about government practices that might not have come out otherwise.

A nonpartisan group, the Political Rights Defense Fund, has helped make that information public. The PRDF has conducted a nationwide drive to win broad support for the civil liberties issues in the case and to raise money for legal and other costs.

The SWP suit is a strong test case. It has produced proof of unjustifiable harassment of a legal political party. The evidence shows that the government is out to disrupt the SWP because it doesn't like the ideas of the SWP. The party doesn't advocate or engage in violent or illegal activity, and never has. The government knows that. FBI officials have admitted it publicly, including to the House Intelligence Committee.

The party's 1976 presidential candidate, Peter Camejo, explained some of the SWP's ideas to the House committee:

We believe that this society needs to be reorganized on the basis of production for human needs, not for private profit. We think that a political party based on the working class is needed. . . . On many issues our views are shared by many, if not most, Americans. These are issues such as the right of every worker to a job, the right of Blacks to attend desegregated schools, the importance of the Equal Rights Amendment, and opposition to sending American soldiers to prop up reactionary governments around the world.

On the question of establishing socialism, however, we are in a minority. Our goal is to win a majority to our point of view.

We run in elections to explain our ideas and win support for our program. In addition, our members participate in organizing demonstrations, such as the large peaceful antiwar marches that helped force an end to the Vietnam war. Many of our members are active in the labor movement and the struggle to desegregate the schools. We hold public meetings and distribute leaflets, books, and newspapers. These are all activities protected by the Bill of Rights.

The case is also breaking some new legal ground. For one thing, the government's use of informers in political organizations is unconstitutional, and should be outlawed. In a political group in which every member is expected to be an activist of some sort, every informer, hostile to the aims and purposes of the group, is bound to be a provocateur.

Informers don't just passively take notes. They *act*. And they act out of their loyalty to the FBI, not to the political group. Therefore, informers interfere with the freedom of speech and association of those members who have the best interests of the organization at heart. (The FBI recently admitted that one of the informers on its payroll, posing as a socialist, even ran for public office in 1972.)

Also, the suit challenges the government's right to censor those files it is forced to release. The FBI is still keeping secret some of the most damning parts of the files—the government's use of burglary, wiretapping, mail tampering, and other illegal tactics.

Now the main task is exposing the fact that the government's unconstitutional political harassment continues. Even though government officials say Cointelpro ended in April 1971, the truth is that harassment—and the government's attempts to justify it—go on.

The SWP recently forced the FBI to release files showing use of Cointelpro techniques well after April 1971. And as part of the evidence in the socialists' case, the Political Rights Defense Fund has gathered reports of more than 225 incidents of harassment that took place *after* 1971.

There have been months of revelations, Congressional hearings, commissions, recommendations, and administrative guidelines. But the government hasn't outlawed or abolished the abuses of the FBI and CIA. Just the opposite: for one thing, new Justice Department guidelines allow the FBI to open "investigations" on any group whose activities "will involve the use of force or violence." Of course, the FBI remains the one to predict what a group or individual "will" do. The only possible purpose or effect of any such guideline is to allow the FBI to spy on just about any group or demonstration it wants to.

The glare of public attention has forced these agencies to try to justify their continuing operations. The FBI, for example, says that it is now just "investigating" crime and possible future crime. That, of course, is not true. A top bureau official was more candid when he testified before the House Intelligence Committee. Asked why the FBI subjected the Socialist Workers party to endless harassment, he said, "I regard the SWP as a party that follows the doctrine of Marxism-Leninism as interpreted by Leon Trotsky." That, however, is not a crime.

The lawyer defending the government against the SWP suit was also fairly candid during a courtroom clash in late 1974. He was trying to justify the FBI's intention to send spies to a national convention of the Young Socialist Alliance. As his "evidence" he read the judge quotations from Marx's *Communist Manifesto* of 1848!

As late as March 1976, the FBI stated as one of its current official policy reasons for "investigating" members and suspected members of the Socialist Workers party: ". . . the FBI is concerned that members of subversive groups will, at some future time, gain responsible positions not only in Government but also in industry and education."

The FBI in 1976 asserts the right to keep track of people engaged in legal political activity to prevent them from getting and keeping jobs. That is an exact parallel to the Cointelpro operations that government officials insist were discontinued in 1971.

The first step in stopping the crimes of the FBI and the CIA is to get the full truth before the American people. The suits and civil liberties efforts that caused the exposure of the documents printed here are helping to do that.

Cathy Perkus
Political Rights
Defense Fund

CONTENTS

Introduction

Beginning in the fall of 1971, some curious events took place in Detroit, Michigan. In late October, lists of supporters, contributors, and subscribers to the party newspaper were stolen from the campaign headquarters of the Michigan Socialist Workers party. A few months later, the home of a Socialist Workers party organizer was robbed. Valuables were ignored, but membership lists and internal party bulletins were stolen. The burglaries remain unsolved.

If we ask who might be interested in obtaining the stolen material, a plausible hypothesis suggests itself. The natural hypothesis gains support from the fact that persons whose names appeared on the stolen lists were then contacted and harassed by FBI agents, and a member's confidential letter of resignation from the party, apparently stolen from headquarters, was transmitted by the FBI to the Civil Service Commission. Information that has since been obtained about FBI activities, including burglaries over many years, lends further substantiation to the conclusion that the FBI was engaged in one of its multifarious endeavors to undermine and disrupt activities that fall beyond the narrow bounds of the established political consensus.

The Detroit events recall another incident which, with its aftermath, became the major news story of 1974. But it would be misleading to compare the Detroit burglaries to the Watergate caper, If, indeed, the FBI was responsible, as seems most likely, then the Detroit burglaries are a far more serious matter. If the conclusion is correct, then in Detroit it was the political police of the national government which, in their official function, were engaged in disrupting the "sanctity of the democratic process,"

3

not merely a gang of bunglers working "outside the system." The ousting of Richard Nixon for his misdeeds was described in the nation's press as "a stunning vindication of our constitutional system." [1] The Detroit example, and others far more serious to which I return, suggest a rather different reaction. There is a fundamental distinction between Watergate and Detroit. In the case of the events surrounding Watergate, the victims were men of power who are expected to share in the ruling of society and the formation of ideology. In Detroit the victims were outsiders, fair game for political repression of a sort that is quite normal. Thus it is true, in a sense, that the punishment of Nixon and his cohorts was a vindication of our system, as this system actually operates in practice. The Nixon gang had broken the rules, directing against the political center a minor variant of the techniques of repression that are commonly applied against radical dissent. If the basic work of repression continues, after Nixon, without appreciable comment or concern, then this too will show that the system is functioning, quite in accord with ample historical precedent.

Assuming FBI involvement, the Detroit incident is nevertheless minor in comparison with other facts exposed during the past several years. From December 1973, the government was compelled through several civil suits to release documentary evidence concerning its various campaigns to undermine and disrupt legal activities directed to social change or simply protest against state policy, through the decade of the 1960s. In comparison with these revelations, the whole Watergate affair was a tea party. The documents and depositions made public during this period, and revelations by disaffected government agents, lay bare a systematic and extensive program of terror, disruption, intimidation, and instigation of violence, initiated under the most liberal Democratic administrations and carried further under Nixon. The Department of Justice, in its apologetic and fragmentary review, asserts that the "counterintelligence program" (Cointelpro) operations "were apparently not reported to any of the Attorneys General in office during the periods in which they were implemented," apart from "certain aspects of the Bureau's efforts to penetrate and disrupt the Communist Party USA and White Hate Groups." [2] Assuming this assertion to be true, we may still observe that government officials who had even a passing familiarity with FBI practices in the past had a definite responsibility to determine how the bureau was acting, under their authority. A review of these programs demonstrates the relative insignificance of the charges raised against Nixon and his associates, specifically, the charges presented in the Congressional Articles of Impeachment.[3] Further insight into the state of American society can be derived by the following simple exercise: compare the attention focused on the Watergate episodes by the mass media, including the liberal press and journals of opinion, with the reaction to the exposures, during exactly the same period, of the FBI programs. This exercise will demonstrate that until the dust had settled over Watergate, there was virtually no mention of the government programs of violence and disruption or comment concerning them, and even after the Watergate affair was successfully concluded, there has been only occasional discussion. The *New Republic*, which during the Watergate period could fairly be considered the semiofficial organ of American liberalism, was unconcerned by these exposures, though hardly an issue passed without a denunciation of Nixon for his crimes, trivial by comparison. With a few honorable exceptions (specifically, the *Nation*), the same was true more generally. The Watergate affair thus reveals quite clearly the subservience of the media to power and official ideology. The example is a particularly telling one, given that the media are so commonly hailed for their courage and independence during this period.

The lesson of Watergate is simple. American liberalism and the corporate media will defend themselves against attack. But their spirited acts of self-defense are not to be construed as a commitment to civil liberties or democratic principle, despite noble and self-serving rhetoric. Quite the contrary. They demonstrate a commitment to the principle that power must not be threatened or injured. The narrow "elites" that control the economy, political life, and the system of conventional doctrine must be immune to the means of harassment that are restricted, in the normal course of events, to those who raise a serious challenge to ruling ideology or state policy or established privilege. An "enemies list" that includes major corporate leaders, media figures, and government intellectuals is an obscenity that is seen shaking the foundations of the republic. The involvement of the national political police in the assassination of Black Panther leaders, however, barely deserves comment in the national press, including the liberal press and journals, with rare exceptions.

The Cointelpro operations of the 1960s were modeled on the successful programs of earlier years undertaken to disrupt the American Communist party. Though details are unknown, these programs were no secret, and were generally regarded as legitimate. The programs directed against the Communist party continued through the 1960s, with such interesting innovations as Operation Hoodwink from 1966 through mid-1968, designed to incite organized crime against the Communist party through documents fabricated by the FBI, evidently in the hope that criminal elements would carry on the work of repression and disruption in their own manner, by means that may be left to the imagination.[4]

From the evidence now available, it appears that the first FBI disruption program (apart from the CP) was launched in August 1960 against groups advocating independence for Puerto Rico. In October 1961, the "SWP Disruption Program" was put into operation against the Socialist Workers party. The grounds offered, in a secret FBI memorandum, were the following: the party had been "openly espousing its line on a local national basis through running candidates for public office and strongly directing and/or supporting such causes as Castro's Cuba and integration problems . . . in the South." The SWP Disruption Program, put into operation during the Kennedy administration, reveals very clearly the FBI's understanding of its function: to block legal political activity that departs from orthodoxy, to disrupt opposition to state policy, to undermine the civil rights movement.

These basic commitments were pursued in subsequent years. For example, the Phoenix office of the FBI noted in a memorandum of October 1, 1968, that Professor Morris Starsky of Arizona State University, "by his actions, has continued to spotlight himself as a target for counterintelligence action." These "actions" consisted of the following crimes against the state: "He and his wife were both named as presidential electors by and for the Socialist Workers Party when the SWP in August, 1968, gained a place on the ballot in Arizona. In addition they have signed themselves as treasurer and secretary respectively of the Arizona SWP." Nothing further is alleged, though an earlier memorandum (May 31, 1968) identifies Starsky as one of those who have provided "inspiration and leadership" for "New Left organizations and activities in the Phoenix metropolitan area," so that he is one of "the most logical targets for potential counterintelligence action." The memorandum suggests that "reliable and cooperative contracts in the mass media" should be helpful in this particular program of "Disruption of the New Left." The documents in the Starsky case also indicate that prior to the targeting of Starsky on October 1, the FBI had somehow influenced the Board of Regents that controls the university to "find cause to separate Professor STARSKY from the public payroll" on trumped-up charges.[5]

Similarly, the comprehensive program to "expose, disrupt, and otherwise neutralize the activities of the various New Left organizations, their leadership and adherents," secretly put into operation in May 1968, was motivated by the fact that New Left activists 'urge revolution," are responsible for unspecified "violence and disruption," "call for the defeat of the United States in Vietnam," and "continually and falsely allege police brutality and do not hesitate to utilize unlawful acts to further their so-called causes." They have even "on many occasions viciously and scurrilously attacked the Director and the Bureau in an attempt to hamper our investigation of it and to drive us off the college campuses," where, naturally, the state's political police should be free to operate with impunity. The latter offense was particularly grave since, as is now known, FBI provocateurs were engaged in extensive efforts throughout the country to instigate campus violence, disrupt student groups, eliminate radical faculty, and the like, and FBI agents were, for example, engaged in such actions as stealing documents from campus groups and burglarizing the offices of professors supporting them.[6]

The commitment of the FBI to undermine the civil rights movement, despite an elaborate pretense to the contrary (and even some actions as government policy vacillated on the issue), will come as no surprise to people with first-hand experience in the South in the early 1960s. As late as summer 1965, FBI observers refused to act within their legal authority to protect civil rights demonstrators who were being savagely beaten by police and thrown into stockades. (Some who tried to find sanctuary on federal property were thrown from the steps of the federal building in Jackson, Mississippi, by federal marshals.) These efforts continued in later years, as, for example, when the FBI, under Cointelpro, succeeded in driving a Black minister from the Jackson Human Rights Project in early 1969, causing him to leave the South altogether, by sending him a "spurious, threatening letter" and encouraging school and church officials to file complaints against him on the basis of charges which (according to his ACLU lawyer) were fabricated by the bureau and "derogatory" information provided by the bureau.[7]

There is no dearth of other examples to illustrate what the report of the House Select Committee on Intelligence (Pike

Committee) calls "FBI racism." The campaign to discredit Dr. Martin Luther King is an example that is now well known. In October 1963 the FBI sought permission, which was granted by Attorney General Robert Kennedy, to install wiretaps on King's home telephone and at two offices of the Southern Christian Leadership Conference, which King headed. In November 1964 the FBI sent King the following unsigned note:

> King, there is only one thing left for you to do. You know what it is. You have just 34 days in which to do it. (This exact number has been selected for a specific reason.) It has definite practical significance. You are done. There is but one way out for you.

Enclosed was a tape obtained from electronic surveillance. The note was received thirty-four days before Dr. King was to receive the Nobel Peace Prize, and was, quite naturally, taken to be an effort to drive him to suicide. The bureau also harassed the Mississippi Freedom Democratic Party in 1964. In 1969 and 1970 it attempted to destroy two civil rights groups in St. Louis by sending forged letters accusing members of marital infidelity; the bureau took credit for helping to break up the marriage of a white activist, who was forced to curtail her civil rights work, by these means. An FBI memo reads: "While the letter sent by the St. Louis division was probably not the sole cause of this separation, it certainly contributed very strongly." [8] The *St. Louis Post-Dispatch* commented editorially (November 19, 1975) that these disclosures make it "hard to imagine that there was any tactic too sordid for this federal agency to use," referring to the efforts "to undermine the effectiveness of ACTION and the Black Liberators in St. Louis," and the general program of which they were a part.

In still another example of bureau tactics under Cointelpro, revealed in the Pike Committee Report,

> the FBI authorized interfering with a Mellon Foundation decision of whether to give Unity Corporation, a black organization in Pittsburgh, Pennsylvania, a $150,000 grant. The FBI contacted a confidential source within the Mellon Foundation, the grant was denied, and the Unity Corporation subsequently went bankrupt.

Chalk up another victory for law and order. We return directly to examples of "FBI racism" of a considerably more serious nature.

Predictably, the most serious of the FBI disruption programs were those directed against "Black Nationalists." These programs, also initiated under liberal Democratic administrations, had as their purpose "to expose, disrupt, misdirect, discredit, or otherwise neutralize the activities of black nationalist, hate-type organizations and groupings, their leadership, spokesmen, membership, and supporters, and to counter their propensity for violence and civil disorder." Agents were instructed "to inspire action in instances where circumstances warrant." Specifically, they were to undertake actions to discredit these groups both within "the responsible Negro community" and to "Negro radicals," and also "to the white community, both the responsible community and to 'liberals' who have vestiges of sympathy for militant black nationalists simply because they are Negroes. . . ."

Several model actions were proposed to agents, who were instructed "to take an enthusiastic and imaginative approach to this new counterintelligence endeavor," including an action apparently directed against the Student Nonviolent Coordinating Committee (SNCC) in 1967, in which local police, alerted by the FBI, arrested leaders "on every possible charge until they could no longer make bail" so that they "spent most of the summer in jail and no violence traceable to [censored] took place." In this case too, agents were directed to use "established local news media contacts" and other "sources available to the Seat of Government" to "disrupt or neutralize" these organizations and to "ridicule and discredit" them. In the light of these documents, one cannot fail to recall the elaborate subsequent campaign, in this case abetted by several liberal intellectuals and "democratic socialists," to ridicule and discredit individuals who attempted to raise funds for the Black Panthers during the period when they were being subjected to extensive police and judicial attack.

Among the most remarkable of the revelations concerning the FBI campaigns against Black groups are those relating to the attempts to exploit gang warfare and incite murderous attacks, which have now come to light in several cities. A Cointelpro memo mailed November 25, 1968, informs recipient offices that:

> . . . a serious struggle is taking place between the Black Panther Party (BPP) and the US organization. The struggle has reached such proportions that it is taking on the aura of gang warfare with attendant threats of murder and reprisals.
>
> In order to fully capitalize upon BPP and US differences as well as to exploit all avenues of creating further dissension in the ranks of the BPP, recipient offices are instructed to submit imaginative and hard-hitting counterintelligence measures aimed at crippling the BPP.

A series of cartoons were produced in an effort to incite violence between the Black Panther party and US—for example, one showing Panther leader David Hilliard hanging dead with a rope around his neck from a tree, with two US members below, one saying to the other: "HE REALLY WAS A PAPER TIGER," and other comparably imaginative creations. The San Diego office reported to the director (September 18, 1969) that:

> In view of the recent killing of BPP member SYLVESTER BELL, a new cartoon is being considered in the hopes that it will assist in the continuance of the rift between BPP and US. This cartoon, or series of cartoons, will be similar in nature to those formerly approved by the Bureau and will be forwarded to the Bureau for evaluation and approval immediately upon their completion.

Under the heading "TANGIBLE RESULTS" the memo continues as follows:

> Shootings, beatings, and a high degree of unrest continues to prevail in the ghetto area of southeast San Diego. Although no specific counterintelligence action can be credited with contributing to this over-all situation, it is felt that a substantial amount of the unrest is directly attributable to this program.

Under the same headline, the memo reports that "the BPP Breakfast Program appears to be floundering in San Diego due to lack of public support and unfavorable publicity concerning it." The "unfavorable publicity" included anonymous telephone calls placed by the bureau to Auxiliary Bishop [censored] "protesting the BPP Breakfast Program and Father [censored] participation therein." Additional calls were proposed, since earlier ones had proven so effective in blocking this program to distribute free breakfasts to the poor.

The Chicago office was even more imaginative. On January 30, 1969, it received permission, as requested, to mail the following letter to Jeff Fort, leader of the Blackstone Rangers:

> Brother Jeff: I've spent some time with some Panther friends on the west side lately and I know what's been going on. The brothers that run the Panthers blame you for blocking their thing and there's supposed to be a hit out for you. I'm not a Panther, or a Ranger, just black. From what I see these Panthers are out for themselves not black people. I think you ought to know what their up to. I know what I'd do if I was you. You might hear from me again.
>
> A black brother you don't know.

"Their thing" was an attempt by the Panthers to politicize the Blackstone Rangers, described by the Chicago office of the FBI as a group "to whom violent type activity, shooting, and the like, are second nature."

The purpose of the letter was explicitly stated. It was sent "in anticipation that its receipt by Fort will intensify the degree of animosity existing between these two Black extremist organizations." It is obvious how a "violence-prone" gang might be expected to respond to the information that the Black Panther Party had "a hit out" for its leader.

Releasing these documents, the Senate Select Committee on Intelligence (Church Committee) noted that the Chicago office's proposal of December 16, 1968, came shortly after an alleged shooting incident between Rangers and Panthers, though one Ranger reportedly told police that the incident was in fact a meeting "called because the Panthers wanted to ask the Rangers to stop street killings."[9]

The FBI effort to incite gang war and murder in Chicago failed. It seems that the Panthers and Rangers understood very well just what was happening. The Chicago office of the FBI turned to some new ideas, to which we return directly.

The Pike Committee Report cites other examples illustrating FBI programs concerning Black groups. For instance, an anonymous letter was sent to the Black Panther party accusing a member of being a police informant. In yet another, a threatening letter was sent to Huey Newton "purporting to be a follower of Eldridge Cleaver." These were both under Cointelpro. The intent can easily be imagined.

During these years, FBI provocateurs repeatedly urged and initiated violent acts, including forceful disruption of meetings and demonstrations on and off university campuses, attacks on police, bombings, and so on. Meanwhile, government agencies financed, helped organize, and supplied arms to right-wing terrorist groups that carried out fire-bombings, burglaries, and shootings, all with the knowledge of the government agencies responsible [10]—in most cases the FBI, although one right-wing terrorist in Chicago claims that his group was financed and directed in part by the CIA.[11] One FBI provocateur resigned when he was asked to arrange the bombing of a bridge in such a way that the person who placed the booby-trapped bomb would be killed. This was in Seattle, where it was revealed that FBI infiltrators had been engaged in a campaign of arson, terrorism, and bombings of university and civic buildings, and where the

FBI arranged a robbery, entrapping a young Black man who was paid $75 for the job and killed in a police ambush.[12] In another case, an undercover operative who had formed and headed a pro-Communist Chinese organization "at the direction of the bureau" reports that at the Miami Republican convention he incited "people to turn over one of the buses and then told them that if they really wanted to blow the bus up, to stick a rag in the gas tank and light it" (they were unable to overturn the vehicle). The same ex-operative contends that Cointelpro-type operations, allegedly suspended in April 1971, were in fact continuing as late as mid-1974, when he left the bureau's employ.[13]

Many details are now available concerning the extensive campaign of terror and disruption waged by the government during these years, in part through right-wing paramilitary groups organized and financed by the national government but primarily through the much more effective means of infiltration and provocation. In particular, much of the violence on campus can be attributed to government provocateurs. To cite a few examples, the Alabama branch of the ACLU argued in court that in May 1970 an FBI agent "committed arson and other violence that police used as a reason for declaring that university students were unlawfully assembled" [14]—150 students were arrested. The court ruled that the agent's role was irrelevant unless the defense could establish that he was instructed to commit the violent acts, but this was impossible, according to defense counsel, since the FBI and police thwarted his efforts to locate the agent who had admitted the acts to him. William Frapolly, who surfaced as a government informer in the Chicago Eight conspiracy trial, an active member of student and off-campus peace groups in Chicago, "during an antiwar rally at his college, . . . grabbed the microphone from the college president and wrestled him off the stage" and "worked out a scheme for wrecking the toilets in the college dorms . . . as an act of antiwar protest." [15] Many such cases have been exposed throughout the country.

Perhaps the most shocking story concerns the assassination of Fred Hampton and Mark Clark by Chicago police directed by the state's attorney's office on December 4, 1969, in a predawn raid on a Chicago apartment. Hampton, one of the most promising leaders of the Black Panther party, was killed in bed, perhaps drugged. Depositions in a civil suit in Chicago reveal that the chief of Panther security and Hampton's personal bodyguard, William O'Neal, was an FBI infiltrator. O'Neal gave his FBI "contacting agent," Roy Mitchell, a detailed floor plan of the apartment, which Mitchell turned over to the state's attorney's office shortly before the attack, along with "information"—of dubious veracity—that there were two illegal shotguns in the apartment. For his services, O'Neal was paid over $10,000 from January 1969 through July 1970, according to Mitchell's affidavit.

The availability of the floor plan presumably explains why "all the police gunfire went to the inside corners of the apartment, rather than toward the entrances," and undermines still further the pretense by the police that the police barrage was caused by confusion in unfamiliar surroundings that led them to believe, falsely, that they were being fired upon by the Panthers inside.[16]

Agent Mitchell was named by the *Chicago Tribune* as head of the Chicago Cointelpro directed against the Black Panthers and other Black groups. Whether or not this is true, there is now substantial evidence of direct FBI involvement in this gestapo-style political assassination.

O'Neal, incidentally, continued to report to Mitchell after the raid. He was taking part in meetings with the Hampton family and discussions between lawyers and clients, one of many such examples of violation of the lawyer-client relation. To cite another, which did receive considerable publicity, the chief security officer of the American Indian Movement, also a paid FBI informer, "was the only person, other than defendants and lawyers, with regular access to the room in which defense strategy was planned." So valuable were his services during this period that his cash payment from the bureau was raised from $900 to $1,100 a month. "The Government, in a sworn affidavit at the trial, had appeared to contend that it had no informer in the defense ranks." The informer, who came to believe that AIM was, in his words, a "legal, social organization that wasn't doing anything wrong," reports also that he helped lead an armed take-over of a state office building in Iowa, among other tasks performed for the FBI.[17]

There has been no systematic investigation of the FBI campaign against the Black Panther party in Chicago, as part of its nationwide program of political repression. But on the basis of the scattered information that has come to light, it is possible to offer some speculations as to how FBI plotting may have progressed.

The efforts of late 1968 and early 1969 to instigate gang warfare—specifically, to incite the Rangers to murder leaders of the Black Panthers—ended in failure. In subsequent months, it seems that the Panthers began to achieve some success in moving the Blackstone Rangers from criminal activities to political radicalism. Members of the Rangers were living in the apartment where Hampton and Clark were assassinated. Hampton was proving a effective leader, particularly worrisome to the political police because of his express distaste for violence and inflammatory rhetoric and his emphasis on constructive political action. As long as the Rangers were just a criminal gang terrorizing the Black ghetto, they were of little concern to the FBI—except, of course, insofar as their tendency towards violence could be exploited for the FBI's campaign of political repression. But an alliance with the Panthers, particularly under the leadership of some like Fred Hampton, was another matter.

It is possible that such an analysis led the Chicago office of the FBI, operating within the framework of Cointelpro, to set in motion the events of December 4, 1969. This, of course, remains speculation. To determine what truth there may be in this reconstruction, it would be necessary to conduct a serious investigation of FBI attempts to foment murder, violence, and gang warfare, and of the FBI involvement in the police raid on the Panther apartment. Ample evidence exists to warrant such an investigation. Neither the House nor the Senate Select Committee appears to have attempted to draw the evidence together or to pursue it, so far as publicly available evidence indicates. As for the press and journals of opinion, they have demonstrated conclusively that they are much more concerned with tape erasures, tax fraud, illegal donations, and other such monumental and unprecedented crimes, which were seen as virtually bringing fascism to the United States.

A top secret *Special Report* for the president in June 1970 [18] gives some insight into the motivation for the actions undertaken by the government to destroy the Black Panther party. The report describes the party as "the most active and dangerous black extremist group in the United States." It's "hard-core members" were estimated at about 800, but "a recent poll indicates that approximately 25 per cent of the black population has a great respect for the BPP, including 43 per cent of blacks under 21 years of age." On the basis of such estimates of the potential of the party, the repressive agencies of the state proceeded against it to ensure that it did not succeed in organizing as a substantial social or political force. We may add that in this case, government repression proved quite successful.

The same *Special Report* develops the broader motivation for the FBI operations. The intelligence analysis explains that "the movement of rebellious youth known as the 'New Left,' involving and influencing a substantial number of college students, is having a serious impact on contemporary society with a potential for serious domestic strife." The New Left has "revolutionary aims" and an "identification with Marxism-Leninism." It has attempted "to infiltrate and radicalize labor," and after failing "to subvert and control the mass media" has established "a large network of underground publications which serve the dual purpose of an internal communication network and an external propaganda organ." Its leaders have "openly stated their sympathy with the international communist revolutionary movements in South Vietnam and Cuba; and have directed others into activities which support these movements." "Although New Left groups have been responsible for widespread damage to ROTC facilities, for the halting of some weapons-related research, and for the increasing dissent within the military services, the major threat to the internal security of the United States is that directed against the civilian sector of our society."

A review of events in San Diego, submitted to the Church Committee in June 1975 under the auspices of the American Civil Liberties Union Foundation of Southern California and released to the press at that time, gives further insight into the activities of the FBI during the period we are considering.[19] The report, much of which is based on "public admissions of the officers and agents involved, including sworn testimony at various criminal trials and statements given to news reporters and investigators," describes how the FBI managed to convert a disbanded right-wing paramilitary organization (the Minutemen) into the Secret Army Organization (SAO), placing an FBI informant, Howard Godfrey, in a leadership position. Godfrey was paid $250 a month plus expenses. "Between 1967 and 1972, Godfrey, using F.B.I. resources, furnished firearms, explosives, other equipment and funds to the Minutemen and SAO," supplying at least 75 percent of the SAO's operating expenses.[20] An SAO cell directed by Godfrey "engaged in repeated acts of violence and terrorism against the left," all with the knowledge of his FBI superiors. Among these acts were destruction of newspaper offices and book stores, firebombing of cars, distributing of leaflets giving the address of antiwar activist Peter Bohmer "for any of our readers who may care to look up this Red Scum, and say hello," etc. On January 6, 1972, Godfrey and another SAO member fired two shots into Bohmer's house, using a gun that Godfrey had stolen, seriously wounding a young woman. The following day, Godfrey informed his FBI supervisor, Steve Christiansen, and gave him the gun and a jacket worn by the gunman. Christiansen hid the gun in his apartment for six months and destroyed the jacket, concealing the information from the San Diego police under FBI orders. The story of this and other incidents became public in June 1972 when the SAO was finally broken up by police—after the SAO bombed a movie theater where two police officers and many other citizens were present. The FBI succeeded in averting prosecution of Godfrey or any FBI agents, including Christiansen, who was permitted to resign and set off for Utah, where he reports that "The F.B.I. is taking good care of us." The FBI then continued with other illegal intelligence and terror programs directed against Bohmer and associates, including several assassination plots. Not one FBI agent or informer has been prosecuted.

As an interesting sidelight, the report states that "In the spring of 1971, according to a [San Diego State] college employee, F.B.I. agents furnished information about Bohmer to college administrative officials and looked through and copied or made notes on his confidential college personnel files." Bohmer was then an instructor at the college. The college subsequently brought charges against Bohmer, using "information which could only have been furnished by law enforcement agencies." [21] A hearing was held, but before it made its findings, the college president fired Bohmer. The hearing committee ruled in Bohmer's favor and he was reinstated. The college then arranged a second investigation under the auspices of the American Association of University Professors. Bohmer was cleared again, but the chancellor of the California state college system, Glenn Dumke, declared that he would not permit Bohmer to be rehired and ordered a third hearing. Bohmer won again; a unanimous decision declared that he should be rehired. Dumke rejected the hearing's findings and Bohmer was dismissed. This was only one of many political firings during these years.[22] It is now commonly alleged that during what is sometimes called "the time of troubles" the universities were terrorized by left-wing totalitarians. A careful review of the facts would reveal a rather different story.

The record of FBI-organized violence and terror in San Diego was submitted to the Church Committee in June 1975. On January 11, 1976, the *San Diego Union* reported some of this information, leading to denials by FBI Director Clarence Kelley, who, however, "acknowledged today that a leader of an alleged secret paramilitary group set up in California to battle antiwar protestors was a paid F.B.I. informer." [23] On February 2, the San Diego City Council forwarded a resolution to the Church Committee, "urging its members to come to San Diego to conduct hearings." [24] The City Council also ordered an independent local investigation. One council member said he had informed Senate investigators of efforts to restore peace to the Black community at the time when the FBI was attempting to incite gang warfare there. "We were making progress in our efforts to cool things down, at a time when the F.B.I. was trying to increase the strife and bloodshed," he said. The national chairman of the US organization, now a professor at San Diego State, said that US and the Panthers had been negotiating to avoid bloodshed; "then the F.B.I. stepped in and the shooting started." As we see, the FBI effort to provoke gang warfare among Black groups was only a part of a more general program of violence and terror, involving antiwar activists as well.

In summary, during the decade of the 1960s and for a period of unknown duration since (perhaps still continuing), the FBI extended its earlier clandestine operations against the Communist party, committing its resources to undermining the Puerto Rico independence movement, the Socialist Workers party, the civil rights movement, Black nationalist movements, the Ku Klux Klan, segments of the peace movement, the student movement, and the "New Left" in general. The overall allocation of FBI resources during this period is of course unknown. One relevant bit of evidence is provided by the "Media files," stolen from the Media, Pennsylvania, office of the FBI in March 1971 by a group calling itself "the Citizens' Commission to Investigate the FBI," and widely distributed through left and peace movement channels. According to its analysis of the documents in this FBI office, 1 percent were devoted to organized crime, mostly gambling; 30 percent were "manuals, routine forms, and similar procedural matter"; 40 percent were devoted to political surveillance and the like, including two cases involving right-wing groups, ten concerning immigrants, and over 200 on left or liberal groups. Another 14 percent of the documents concerning draft resistance and "leaving the military without government permission." The remainder concerned bank robberies, murder, rape, and interstate theft.[25] In the case of a secret organization like the FBI, we cannot know whether or not these figures are typical. It is clear, however, that the commitment of the FBI to undermine and destroy popular movements that departed from political orthodoxy was extensive, and was apparently proportional to the strength and promise of such movements—as one would expect in the case of the secret police organization of any state, though it is doubtful that there is anything comparable to this record among the Western industrial democracies.

The effectiveness of the state disruption programs is not easy to evaluate. Surely it was not slight. Black leaders estimate the significance of the programs as substantial. Dr. James Turner of Cornell University, president of the African Heritage Studies Association, assesses these programs as having "serious long-term consequences for black Americans," in that they "had created in blacks a sense of depression and hopelessness." [26] He states that "the F.B.I. set out to break the momentum developed in black communities in the late fifties and early sixties"; "we needed to put together organizational mechanisms to deliver services," but instead, "our ability to influence things that happen to us internally and externally was killed." He concludes that "the lack of confidence and paranoia stimulated among black people by these actions" were just beginning to fade. Conceivably, the long-term impact may be salutary: "We realize that we can't depend on symbolism and on inspired leadership and we are beginning to build solidly based organizations." "Symbolism and inspired leadership" are easy targets for the repressive institutions of the state, its propaganda agencies, and cooperative intellectuals. Solidly based organizations may be able to withstand such attacks. The same lesson, of course, must be learned outside the Black community.

We note further that the criminal activities of the FBI were initiated under the liberal Democratic administrations and carried further under Nixon. These programs were (partially) exposed during the Watergate period, and though incomparably more serious than anything charged against Nixon, they were virtually ignored during this period by the liberal national press and journals of opinion. I have discovered personally—and other may verify for themselves—that much of the most significant information is unknown to generally well-informed journalists and other intellectuals, and that the scale of the FBI programs is rarely appreciated, though by now enough information is readily available for those who want to know.

We note finally that "the Justice Department has decided not to prosecute anyone in connection with the Federal Bureau of Investigation's 15-year campaign to disrupt the activities of suspected subversive organizations." [27] J. Stanley Pottinger, head of the Civil Rights Division, reported to the attorney general that he had found "no basis for criminal charges against any particular individuals involving particular incidents." The present director of the FBI has also made clear that he sees nothing particularly serious in the revelations of the past several years. There is as yet no public record or evidence of any systematic investigation of these practices. As already noted, the liberal press paid little heed to the record that was being exposed during the Watergate period, and even since has generally ignored the more serious cases and failed to present anything remotely resembling an accurate picture of the full record and what it implies. In short, the system continues to work.

The criminal programs of the FBI during the 1960's are simply an extension of past practices. As the Pike Committee Report observes, the Socialist Workers party "has been subjected to 34 years of intensive investigation" (and, we may add, years of harassment and disruption as well) without any evidence whatsoever of any illegal activity.[28] According to William C. Sullivan, Hoover's assistant for many years:

Such a very great man as Franklin D. Roosevelt saw nothing wrong in asking the FBI to investigate those opposing his lend-lease policy —a purely political request. He also had us look into the activities of others who opposed our entrance into World War II, just as later Administrations had the FBI look into those opposing the conflict in Vietnam. It was a political request also when he [Roosevelt] instructed us to put a telephone tap, a microphone, and a physical surveillance on an internationally known leader in his Administration. It was done. The results he wanted were secured and given to him. Certain records of this kind . . . were not then or later put into the regular FBI filing system. Rather, they were deliberately kept out of it.[29]

Not long after World War II ended, President Truman put into operation the repressive measures which laid the basis for what is misleadingly called "McCarthyism." The Mundt-Nixon bill calling for the registration of the Communist party was reported out of Nixon's House Committee on Un-American Activities in 1948. Senate liberals objected, and after a Truman veto they proposed as a substitute "the ultimate weapon of repression: concentration camps to intern potential troublemakers on the occasion of some loosely defined future 'Internal Security Emergency'," [30] including, as one case, "insurrection within the United States in aid of a foreign enemy." [31] This substitute was advocated by Benton, Douglas, Graham, Kefauver, Kilgore, Lehman, and Humphrey, then a freshman senator. Humphrey later voted against the bill, though he did not retreat from his concentration camp proposal. In fact, he was concerned that the conference committee had brought back "a weaker bill, not a bill to strike stronger blows at the Communist menace, but weaker blows." The problem with the new bill was that those interned in the detention centers would have "the right of habeas corpus so they can be released and go on to do their dirty business," [32] Humphrey complained. In later years as well Senate liberals were responsible for some of the most repressive legislation.

During the same period, the ideological institutions of American society—the mass media, cinema, and the universities and schools—were successfully purified as radicals were largely eliminated from the sensitive professions and often harassed or dismissed elsewhere as well. It was only under the pressure of the student movement in the late 1960s that the universities were compelled to become slightly less orthodox and to make marginal concessions to freedom of thought and inquiry that moved beyond the ideological consensus determined by ruling groups.

It is now commonly argued that during the late 1960s the universities were virtually taken over by the left, while the mass media took on an adversary position with respect to state authority—some say irresponsibly, while others laud the press for its honesty and independence. This is gross nonsense. The orthodoxy of the universities was barely challenged. Overwhelmingly, university departments, particularly those concerned with domestic policy and international affairs, remained under the control of people committed to the reigning state capitalist ideology, and throughout the Vietnam War the subversion of the universities in the service of state policy persisted with only minor interference. As for the media, I have already pointed out that the Watergate affair—allegedly their finest hour—merely demonstrates their continued subservience to the ruling powers. The same is generally true with regard to the war in Vietnam. Even the liberal press generally continued, to the end, to describe the war as a conflict between North and South Vietnam, hewing close to the official propaganda line. Media doves joined most liberal intellectuals in protesting that the United States was defending South Vietnam in an exercise of misplaced benevolence. The war was "a mistake," a case of good motives transmuted (mysteriously) into bad policy, with no one to blame. The fact that the United States was engaged in direct aggression in South Vietnam, and that its murderous attack against the rural society of South Vietnam then spilled over to neighboring regions, has been consistently suppressed by the media and journals of opinion, again with a few honorable exceptions. The war in Laos and Cambodia was kept "secret" over long periods through the self-censorship of the press, which then hyprocritically blamed Nixon for deception when the time came to punish him for his departure from the established rules of the game. Kissinger's efforts to evade the provisions of the "peace treaty" were also effectively kept from public attention, in a remarkable display of submissiveness. I have given elaborate documentation elsewhere, and will not discuss this matter further here.[33]

When someone suggests a reduction in military spending or the cancellation of some new superweapon development, outraged apologists for militarism are sure to denounce such proposals for "unilateral disarmament." Similarly, a slight breach in orthodoxy is sufficient to terrify authoritarian ideologues, who see in it the collapse of the system of thought control that has been so effective in depoliticizing American society. The gross exaggerations of frightened academics and political commentators serve to illustrate the extent and success of the long-standing system of ideological control in the United States.

I have spoken of this system as a post-World War II phenomenon, but that is misleading. Its roots go far deeper. Recall that J. Edgar Hoover rose to national prominence when he was appointed chief of the General Intelligence (antiradical) division of the Justice Department in August 1919, just before the "Palmer raids" of January 2, 1920, when more than 4,000 alleged "radicals" were rounded up in thirty-three cities in twenty-three states (over 200 aliens were subsequently deported), while the *Washington Post* editorialized that "there is no time to waste on hairsplitting over infringement of liberty" in the face of the Bolshevik menace, and lauded the House of Representatives for its expulsion of socialist congressman Victor Berger on grounds that it could not have given a "finer or more impressive demonstration of Americanism"; the *New York Times* meanwhile described the expulsion of socialist assemblymen as "an American vote altogether, a patriotic and conservative vote" which "an immense majority of the American people will approve and sanction," whatever the benighted electorate may believe.[34]

One may trace the pattern back much further, to the Alien and Sedition Acts by which "the Federalists sought to suppress political opposition and to stamp out lingering sympathy for the principles of the French Revolution,"[35] or the judicial murder of four anarchists for "having advocated doctrines" which allegedly lay behind the explosion of a bomb in Chicago's Haymarket Square after a striker had been killed by police in May 1886.[36]

The Cointelpro documents and the related disclosures are noteworthy, and in accord with historical precedent, in that no specific illegal acts were charged against those "targeted" by the FBI, though a vague "propensity for violence" and unspecified violent acts are alleged. Similarly, the "seditious utterances" of the Haymarket anarchists sufficed, in the eyes of the Chicago police, to attribute "moral responsibility" for the bombing and to justify their prosecution and hanging.[37] And Attorney General Palmer justified his actions "to clean up the country almost unaided by any virile legislation" on grounds of the failure of Congress "to stamp out these seditious societies in their open defiance of law by various forms of propaganda":

> Upon these two basic certainties, first that the "Reds" were criminal aliens, and secondly that the American Government must prevent crime, it was decided that there could be no nice distinctions drawn between the theoretical ideals of the radicals and their actual violations of our national laws. . . .

Palmer's "information showed that communism in this country was an organization of thousands of aliens, who were direct allies of Trotzky." Thus "the Government is now sweeping the nation clean of such alien filth," with the overwhelming support of the press, until they perceived that their own interests were threatened.[38] Elsewhere he described the prisoners as follows:

> Out of the sly and crafty eyes of many of them leap cupidity, cruelty, insanity, and crime; from their lopsided faces, sloping brows, and misshapen features may be recognized the unmistakable criminal type.[39]

Palmer was a liberal and progressive. His purpose was "to tear out the radical seeds that have entangled American ideas in their poisonous theories."[40] His belief that the state has the authority to prevent these seeds from germinating is within the general framework of American liberalism. The mass media, the schools, and the universities defend ideological orthodoxy in their own, generally successful ways. When a threat to reigning dogma is perceived, the state is entitled to act.

After World War I, labor militancy menaced established

privilege. Hoover labored to portray the 1919 steel strike as a "Red conspiracy." A subsequent miner's strike was described by President Wilson as "one of the gravest steps ever proposed in this country," "a grave moral and legal wrong," while the press warned that the miners, "red-soaked in the doctrines of Bolshevism," were "starting a general revolution in America." [41] The Red Scare, as Levin shows, "was promoted, in large part, by major business groups which feared their power was threatened by a leftward trend in the labor movement"; and they had "reason to rejoice" at its substantial success, namely, "to weaken and conservatize the labor movement, to dismantle radical parties, and to intimidate liberals." It "was an attempt—largely successful—to reaffirm the legitimacy of the power elites of capitalism and to further weaken workers' class consciousness." The Red Scare was strongly backed by the press and the American elites until they came to see that their own interests would be harmed as the right-wing frenzy got out of hand—in particular, the anti-immigrant hysteria, which threatened the best reserve of cheap labor.

The Red Scare also served to buttress an interventionist foreign policy. Foster Rhea Dulles observed that "Governmental agencies made most of these fears and kept up a barrage of anti-Bolshevik propaganda throughout 1919 which was at least partially inspired by the need to justify the policy of intervention in both Archangel and Siberia." [42]

After World War II, the story was reenacted. While intellectual ideologists depicted American expansionism as "defense of freedom" (with an occasional, but so understandable excess of zeal), transmuting the brutal Russian state into a global aggressor under an elaborate mythology that even its creators have been compelled to disown, the state moved to ensure obedience and submissiveness to the evolving imperial system and the domestic permanent war economy. As already noted, American liberals had their hand in some of the worst abuses. The general motivation was the traditional one: "there could be no nice distinctions drawn between the theoretical ideals of the radicals and their actual violations of our national laws" (Palmer).

The basic liberal doctrine was laid out clearly by Supreme Court Justice Robert H. Jackson in his opinion upholding the Smith Act on grounds "that it was no violation of free speech to convict Communists for conspiring to teach or advocate the forcible overthrow of the government, even if no clear and present danger could be proved." For if the clear and present danger test were applied, Jackson argued, "it means that Communist plotting is protected during its period of incubation; its preliminary stages of organization and preparation are immune from the law; the Government can move only after imminent action is manifest, when it would, of course, be too late." Thus there must be "some legal formula that will secure an existing order against revolutionary radicalism. . . . There is no constitutional right to 'gang up' on the Government." Opposition tendencies, however minuscule, must be nipped in the bud prior to "imminent action." As for the Communist party, "ordinary conspiracy principles" suffice to charge any individual associated with it "with responsibility for and participation in all that makes up the Party's program" and "even an individual," acting alone and apart from any "conspiracy," "cannot claim that the Constitution protects him in advocating or teaching overthrow of government by force or violence. . . ." [43]

In conformity with these doctrines, the ideological institutions must be kept free of contamination. Even a single tenured Marxist professor of economics in a country as complex and diverse as the United States constitutes a potential threat. As in the case of the Red Scare of 1920, it was only when the hysteria that had been whipped up began to endanger major institutions and individuals near the center of power that the economic and political leadership and their intellectual spokesmen took effective measures to terminate the repression—or more accurately, to restrict it to the proper victims.

Given the historical context, it is entirely natural that the beginnings of the ferment of protest and organization in the early 1960s set the apparatus of repression into operation once again, in the manner described in the documents presented below and elsewhere. Nor is it surprising that American liberalism looked the other way, until the repression struck home under Nixon; and even then, it is important to emphasize once again, indignation was largely restricted to Nixon's crimes, insignificant in comparison to the revelations of the same period. Matters are no different when the Black anarchist Martin Sostre—designated as a "prisoner of conscience" by Amnesty International—was mercilessly persecuted by the state for many years, or when Black students were murdered at Orangeburg and Jackson State, and on and on.

Some commentators have found it "puzzling" that the FBI should devote such energies to hounding a scoutmaster in Orange, New Jersey, whose wife is a socialist, or to disrupting small socialist parties, while "crime rates in American cities escalated and organized crime expanded its interests" and "the real espionage dangers from the Soviet K.G.B." were "apparently ignored." [44] Placing the events in their historical and doctrinal context, the puzzle is easily resolved. The real threat to the "existing order" is not organized crime or the KGB, but "revolutionary radicalism" or even protest by popular groups that have escaped the control of the political leadership and intellectual ideologists. That this threat can quickly become real indeed was made evident in the late 1960s, when American aggression in Vietnam was significantly hampered [45] and its ideological props swept away (in significant circles, though not in the major ideological institutions).

For the most part, however, the threat of intellectual independence and uncontrolled political and social organization has been well contained (the major postwar success of the "containment policy"). Alone among the parliamentary democracies, the United States has had no mass-based socialist party, however mild and reformist, no socialist voice in the media, and virtually no departure from centrist ideology within the schools and universities, at least until the pressure of student activism impelled a slight departure from orthodoxy. All of this is testimony to the effectiveness of the system of controls that has been in force for many years, the activities of the FBI being only the spearhead for far more extensive, substantial, and effective—if more low-keyed—measures enforced throughout American society.

From its inception, the FBI has operated on the liberal doctrine that "preliminary stages of organization and preparation" must be frustrated, well before there is any clear and present danger of "revolutionary radicalism," occasionally progressing beyond the intended bounds of this doctrine. The people of the United States pay dearly for domestic privilege and the securing of imperial domains. The vast waste of social wealth, miserable urban ghettos, meaningless work within authoritarian capitalist institutions, the threat (or reality) of loss of even the opportunity to rent oneself to the owners of capital, standards of health and social welfare that should be intolerable in a society with vast productive resources—all of this must be endured and even welcomed as "the price of freedom" if "the existing order" is to stand without challenge. The intelligentsia have generally played their natural role, promulgating the required doctrines with enthusiasm and energy and diverting or diluting any serious departure from the conventional system of beliefs, with an occasional show of dismay when privileged groups themselves are threatened. As for the state instruments of repression, one can expect little change in coming years, at least until the rise of mass-based popular organizations devoted to social change and to an end of oppression and injustice.

NOAM CHOMSKY
July 1975
Revised, February 1976

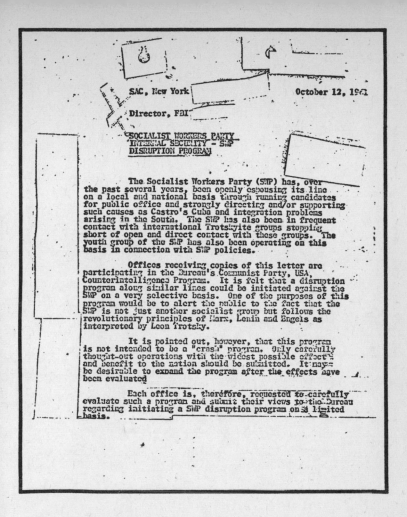

SAC, New York   October 12, 1961

Director, FBI

SOCIALIST WORKERS PARTY
INTERNAL SECURITY - SWP
DISRUPTION PROGRAM

    The Socialist Workers Party (SWP) has, over the past several years, been openly espousing its line on a local and national basis through running candidates for public office and strongly directing and/or supporting such causes as Castro's Cuba and integration problems arising in the South. The SWP has also been in frequent contact with international Trotskyite groups stopping short of open and direct contact with these groups. The youth group of the SWP has also been operating on this basis in connection with SWP policies.

    Offices receiving copies of this letter are participating in the Bureau's Communist Party, USA, Counterintelligence Program. It is felt that a disruption program along similar lines could be initiated against the SWP on a very selective basis. One of the purposes of this program would be to alert the public to the fact that the SWP is not just another socialist group but follows the revolutionary principles of Marx, Lenin and Engels as interpreted by Leon Trotsky.

    It is pointed out, however, that this program is not intended to be a "crash" program. Only carefully thought-out operations with the widest possible effect and benefit to the nation should be submitted. It may be desirable to expand the program after the effects have been evaluated

    Each office is, therefore, requested to carefully evaluate such a program and submit their views to the Bureau regarding initiating a SWP disruption program on a limited basis.

1961 FBI letter initiating the Socialist Workers Party Disruption Program. It cites the party's electoral activities, defense of Cuba, and support for the civil rights movement, not any alleged violent or illegal actions.

The faculty and a great majority of the students at the school were very distressed and upset with the foolish and extremist activities of JACKSON and his associates, as was evidenced by the forming of the Defense Committee. Additionally, they felt that the programs of the BPP and its representatives and associates was a program of nihilism.

III. PROPOSED COUNTERINTELLIGENCE MEASURE

It is proposed that the following letter be typewritten on commercial paper and forwarded to DONALD JACKSON at his Hillcrest Street residence at Tougaloo, Mississippi, bearing Tougaloo, Mississippi, postmark:

"Tougaloo College
Tougaloo, Mississippi

Date

"Muhammed Kenyatta---

"The deplorable activities and conduct of you and your Black Panther brothers at the recently completed Black Spring Weekend have shocked the Tougaloo College community into realizing the basic errors in the intimidation methods and nihilistic doctrines which you promote. Your immature actions of discharging firearms near the campus on Saturday afternoon, April 11, further alienated you and you 'outsiders' from the spirit and tone in which all desired the BSW to take. Your recent involvement in various criminal activities in and near Tougaloo College as well as your irresponsibility in paying your school bills while at Tougaloo College further exemplify the inappropriateness of you, of all people, in any manner acting as a representative of blacks in Mississippi or anywhere for that matter. Your conduct and demeanor is representative of traits and habits we in our quest are trying to rise above.

Pages 28 and 29: Among the fifty pages of Muhammad Kenyatta's Cointelpro file is this letter warning the civil rights leader to leave Mississippi or face measures "which

"Accordingly, it has been determined by solidity representative elements of the Tougaloo College Student Body that you are directed to remain away from this campus until such time as your conduct and general demeanor reach the desired level. This directive also applies to your bringing any of your unruly and undisciplined associates to the campus.

"Should you feel that this is a hollow directive and not heed our diplomatic and well thought out warning we shall consider contacting local authorities regarding some of your activities or take other measures available to us which would have a more direct effect and which would not be as cordial as this note.

"Tougaloo College Defense Committee

IV. OBJECTIVE

It is hoped that this letter, if approved and forwarded to JACKSON, will give him the impression that he has been discredited at the Tougaloo College campus and is no longer welcomed there. It could discourage him from inviting out of state extremists to visit him and while here to speak at Tougaloo College. It may possibly also cause him to decide to leave Mississippi and return to his original home in Pennsylvania.

V. RECOMMENDATION.

would have a more direct effect." The threat is attributed to Tougaloo students.

SAC, Albany

August 25, 1967

Director, FBI

COUNTER INTELLIGENCE PROGRAM
BLACK NATIONALIST - HATE GROUPS
INTERNAL SECURITY

Offices receiving copies of this letter are instructed
to immediately establish a control file, captioned as above, and
to assign responsibility for following and coordinating this new
counterintelligence program to an experienced and imaginative
Special Agent well versed in investigations relating to black
nationalist, hate-type organizations. The field office control
file used under this program may be maintained in a pending
inactive status until such time as a specific operation or
technique is placed under consideration for implementation.

The purpose of this new counterintelligence endeavor
is to expose, disrupt, misdirect, discredit, or otherwise
neutralize the activities of black nationalist, hate-type
organizations and groupings, their leadership, spokesmen,
membership, and supporters, and to counter their propensity for
violence and civil disorder. The activities of all such groups
of intelligence interest to this Bureau must be followed on a
continuous basis so we will be in a position to promptly take
advantage of all opportunities for counterintelligence and to
inspire action in instances where circumstances warrant. The
pernicious background of such groups, their duplicity, and devious
maneuvers must be exposed to public scrutiny where such publicity
will have a neutralizing effect. Efforts of the various groups/

Pages 30-32: First page of a memo from J. Edgar Hoover, dated August 25, 1967, that put into effect the Cointelpro-Black Nationalist Hate Groups. It announced that the purpose of the new disruption program was "to expose, disrupt, misdirect, discredit, or otherwise neutralize" the Black movement. The next two documents, from a March 4, 1968 memo in the same Cointelpro, elaborate on the program's

nationalist activity, and interested in counterintelligence,
to coordinate this program. This Agent will be responsible
for the periodic progress letters being requested, but each
Agent working this type of case should participate in the
formulation of counterintelligence operations.

GOALS

For maximum effectiveness of the Counterintelligence
Program, and to prevent wasted effort, long-range goals are
being set.

1. Prevent the coalition of militant black
nationalist groups. In unity there is strength; a truism
that is no less valid for all its triteness. An effective
coalition of black nationalist groups might be the first
step toward a real "Mau Mau" in America, the beginning of
a true black revolution.

2. Prevent the rise of a "messiah" who could
unify, and electrify, the militant black nationalist movement.
███████ might have been such a "messiah;" he is the martyr
of the movement today. ███████████████████████████
██████████ all aspire to this position. ██████████████
███████ is less of a threat because of his age. ███████ could
be a very real contender for this position should he abandon
his supposed "obedience" to "white, liberal doctrines"
(nonviolence) and embrace black nationalism. ███████████
has the necessary charisma to be a real threat in this way.

3. Prevent violence on the part of black
nationalist groups. This is of primary importance, and is,
of course, a goal of our investigative activity; it should
also be a goal of the Counterintelligence Program. Through
counterintelligence it should be possible to pinpoint potential
troublemakers and neutralize them before they exercise their
potential for violence.

4. Prevent militant black nationalist groups and
leaders from gaining respectability, by discrediting them
to three separate segments of the community. The goal of
discrediting black nationalists must be handled tactically
in three ways. You must discredit these groups and
individuals to, first, the responsible Negro community.
Second, they must be discredited to the white community,

purpose. The names of Malcolm X, Martin Luther King, Jr.,
and Stokely Carmichael fit in the censored spaces in goal 2.
This file raised questions about FBI complicity in the
murders of Malcolm X and Dr. King. The memo was issued
one month before King was killed. Other Cointelpro files
show that the FBI also had infiltrators in Malcolm's Muslim
Mosque, Inc. (see chapter 5).

both the responsible community and to "liberals" who have
vestiges of sympathy for militant black nationalist simply
because they are Negroes. Third, these groups must be
discredited in the eyes of Negro radicals, the followers
of the movement. This last area requires entirely different
tactics from the first two. Publicity about violent tendencies
and radical statements merely enhances black nationalists
to the last group; it adds "respectability" in a different
way.

5. A final goal should be to prevent the long-
range growth of militant black nationalist organizations,
especially among youth. Specific tactics to prevent these
groups from converting young people must be developed.

Besides these five goals counterintelligence is
a valuable part of our regular investigative program as it
often produces positive information.

TARGETS

Primary targets of the Counterintelligence Program,
Black Nationalist-Hate Groups, should be the most violent
and radical groups and their leaders. We should emphasize
those leaders and organizations that are nationwide in scope
and are most capable of disrupting this country. These
targets should include the radical and violence-prone
leaders, members, and followers of the:

Offices handling these cases and those of
should be alert for counterintelligence suggestions.

INSTRUCTIONS

Within 30 days of the date of this letter each office
should:

1. Advise the Bureau of the identity of the Special
Agent assigned to coordinate this program.

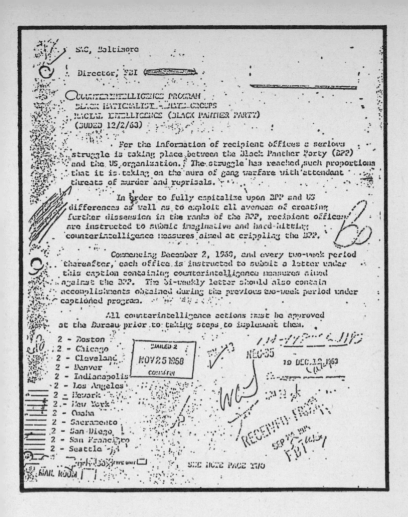

Pages 33-35: "As a result of our efforts the Black Panther
party in San Diego is no more. It has been completely done
away with."—the San Diego office of the FBI boasted in a
memo to J. Edgar Hoover early in 1970. The bureau sent
to the Panthers these derogatory cartoons that appear to
have been prepared by the US organization. Similar derisive
posters, trying to capitalize on political differences between
the Panthers and US, were tacked on walls and telephone
poles in San Diego. These files raise questions about FBI
links to the murders of six Panthers and the wounding of
four other Black activists in San Diego.

HE REALLY WAS A PAPER TIGER

Detailed FBI floor plan of the Chicago apartment where Panther leaders Fred Hampton and Mark Clark were killed by police in 1969. An FBI agent made the drawing from information supplied by Hampton's bodyguard—who later surfaced as a bureau informer—and passed it on to Chicago police less than two weeks before the killings. A court ordered the files released in response to a suit by the victims' families and seven survivors of the raid.

Memorandum

TO : Mr. W. C. Sullivan   DATE: 10-9-69

FROM : C. D. Brennan

SUBJECT: SOCIALIST WORKERS PARTY (SWP)
INTERNAL SECURITY - SOCIALIST WORKERS PARTY
DISRUPTION PROGRAM

Purpose:

     To secure approval for discontuance of our disruptive program against the SWP to eliminate paper work.

Observations:

     Captioned program was initiated on October 12, 1961, to cause disruption within the SWP and to alert the public to the organization's subversive character. Prior to October, 1967, this program was supervised as an adjunct of the Bureau's counterintelligence program directed against the communists, the Klan, and hate-type groups. Currently, this program is being supervised by the substantive desk responsible for handling the investigation of the SWP. Field is not required to submit status letters and potential counterintelligence actions are handled on an individual basis.

     Since the last evaluation of this program in October, 1968, four proposals have been considered with three being approved by the Bureau. No significant tangible results have been reported to date.

RECOMMENDATION:

     In order to eliminate paper work wherever possible, it is recommended that captioned disruptive action be discontinued as a program. In the future, the disruptive action directed against the SWP will be handled on an individual case basis as deemed appropriate.

1 - Mr. W. C. Sullivan
1 - Mr. C. D. Brennan
1 - Mr. L. A. Crescioli

LAC:kle
(4)

Memos that ostensibly discontinued Cointelpro are worded unmistakably to allow future disruption. This one, dated October 10, 1969, recommends getting rid of the title "SWP Disruption Program" to "eliminate paper work," and adds: "In the future, the disruption action directed against the SWP will be handled on an individual case basis as deemed appropriate."

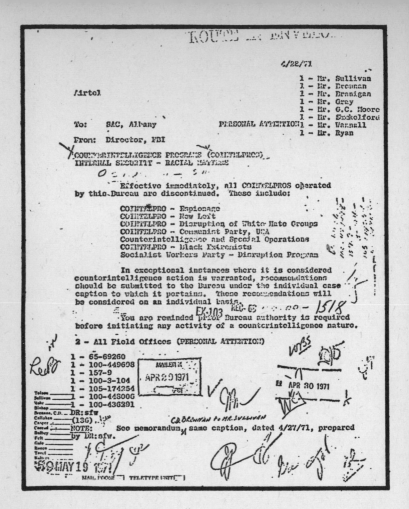

4/28/71

1 - Mr. Sullivan
1 - Mr. Brennan
1 - Mr. Branigan
1 - Mr. Gray
1 - Mr. G.C. Moore
1 - Mr. Shackelford
1 - Mr. Vannall
1 - Mr. Ryan

Airtel

To: SAC, Albany   PERSONAL ATTENTION

From: Director, FBI

COUNTERINTELLIGENCE PROGRAMS (COINTELPRO)
INTERNAL SECURITY - RACIAL MATTERS

        Effective immediately, all COINTELPROS operated
by this Bureau are discontinued. These include:

        COINTELPRO - Espionage
        COINTELPRO - New Left
        COINTELPRO - Disruption of White Hate Groups
        COINTELPRO - Communist Party, USA
        Counterintelligence and Special Operations
        COINTELPRO - Black Extremists
        Socialist Workers Party - Disruption Program

        In exceptional instances where it is considered
counterintelligence action is warranted, recommendations
should be submitted to the Bureau under the individual case
caption to which it pertains. These recommendations will
be considered on an individual basis.

        You are reminded prior Bureau authority is required
before initiating any activity of a counterintelligence nature.

        2 - All Field Offices (PERSONAL ATTENTION)

1 - 65-69260
1 - 100-449698
1 - 157-9
1 - 100-3-104
1 - 105-174254
1 - 100-448006
1 - 100-436291

DR:sfw
(136)
NOTE: See memorandum, same caption, dated 4/27/71, prepared
by DR:sfw.

MAIL ROOM □   TELETYPE UNIT □

Pages 38 and 39: 1971 documents purporting to end seven counterintelligence programs allude to the break-in at the Media, Pennsylvania, FBI office which shattered their secrecy. The programs "should now be discontinued for

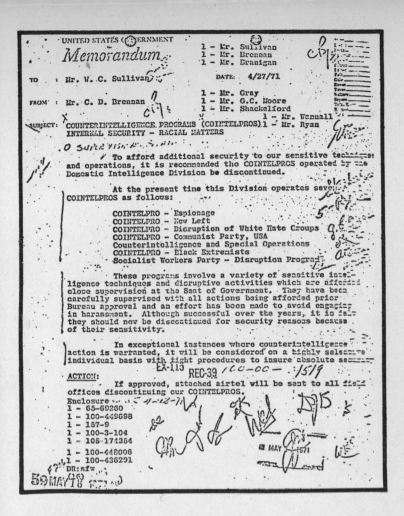

UNITED STATES GOVERNMENT

Memorandum

1 - Mr. Sullivan
1 - Mr. Brennan
1 - Mr. Branigan

TO : Mr. W. C. Sullivan   DATE: 4/27/71

FROM : Mr. C. D. Brennan

1 - Mr. Gray
1 - Mr. G.C. Moore
1 - Mr. Shackelford
1 - Mr. Wannall
1 - Mr. Ryan

SUBJECT: COUNTERINTELLIGENCE PROGRAMS (COINTELPROS)
INTERNAL SECURITY - RACIAL MATTERS

To afford additional security to our sensitive techniques and operations, it is recommended the COINTELPROS operated by the Domestic Intelligence Division be discontinued.

At the present time this Division operates seven COINTELPROS as follows:

COINTELPRO - Espionage
COINTELPRO - New Left
COINTELPRO - Disruption of White Hate Groups
COINTELPRO - Communist Party, USA
Counterintelligence and Special Operations
COINTELPRO - Black Extremists
Socialist Workers Party - Disruption Program

These programs involve a variety of sensitive intelligence techniques and disruptive activities which are afforded close supervision at the Seat of Government. They have been carefully supervised with all actions being afforded prior Bureau approval and an effort has been made to avoid engaging in harassment. Although successful over the years, it is felt they should now be discontinued for security reasons because of their sensitivity.

In exceptional instances where counterintelligence action is warranted, it will be considered on a highly selective individual basis with tight procedures to insure absolute security.

EX-113   REC-39 100-00 - 1519

ACTION:
If approved, attached airtel will be sent to all field offices discontinuing our COINTELPROS.

Enclosure
1 - 65-69260
1 - 100-449698
1 - 157-9
1 - 100-3-104
1 - 105-174354
1 - 100-448006
1 - 100-436291
DR:sfw

59 MAY 18 1971

MAY 4 1971

---

security reasons," but disruptive tactics will continue "on a highly selective individual basis with tight procedures to insure absolute secrecy."

1 "Prevent these people from getting elected"

In late 1971 Donald Segretti was discharged from the army, where he had served as an attorney. He had a friend in the White House and he quickly landed a new job.

In the next few months strange things began to happen to some of the candidates for the Democratic presidential nomination. During the New Hampshire primary the state's major newspaper printed a letter accusing Edmund Muskie of making derogatory statements about French-Americans. Sometime later it would be discovered that the letter was a phony, but two weeks before election day it sparked quite a stir.

Later, there were fake press releases issued on the stationery of Muskie and Hubert Humphrey.

Then, on June 17, 1972, five men were discovered breaking into the headquarters of the Democratic National Committee at the Watergate complex in Washington, D.C. The story that eventually unraveled—including spying and political sabotage—had an unprecedented impact on American political life. It eventually forced the resignation of the president of the United States.

The Cointelpro documents reveal that none of the Watergate crimes was original. For years, the FBI has used every one of the plumbers' "dirty tricks"—and worse—against civil rights leaders, antiwar activists, others on the government's "enemies list," and the Socialist Workers party.

As this country's political police, the FBI has been assigned the role of determining what ideas are fit for the American people to hear and what ideas are not. Socialism, in their opinion, is not fit.

The ruling class, which runs the government, is convinced that it would be better for them if socialism were considered illegitimate or "subversive." The idea that the working people of this country should take over its wealth and resources and use them for their own welfare is a subversive idea—if you are a capitalist.

In the early 1960s the witch-hunt that had dominated American politics during the 1950s was giving way to a greater openness to radical ideas. Socialists began winning a place on the ballot—and were more and more being treated as legitimate candidates with a particular point of view. The FBI decided that they had a problem. Cointelpro was their solution.

The Cointelpro plot to disrupt election campaigns was concocted not because of any illegal activities by the SWP, but because, as J. Edgar Hoover said, socialist candidates were "openly" talking to people about their ideas.

The documents at the end of this chapter show that the FBI attempted to wreck the 1961 campaign of a Black socialist for Manhattan borough president, waged a sustained drive against Clifton DeBerry, the SWP's 1964 presidential candidate, tried to get socialists excluded from supporting an independent Black candidate in San Francisco in 1964, and incited an attack on Fred Halstead when he was the SWP presidential candidate in 1968.

These actions are only part of the record of FBI sabotage against socialist candidates. And there are operations that remain hidden in files the FBI is refusing to disclose.

One Cointelpro operation that has come to light through the socialists' suit concerns the 1966 campaign of Judy White for governor of New York. This was during the period when the antiwar movement was beginning to have a major impact on the thinking of the American people. White was a leader of the antiwar movement.

A broad layer of opponents of the war—including many radicals who were not particularly close to the SWP—had endorsed White as the only antiwar candidate in the race.

Campaign supporters worked hard to get the signatures necessary to obtain ballot status, which brought a significant amount of attention from the media.

The FBI looked for a way to sabotage this campaign. They noticed that according to New York law White was formally not old enough to hold the office of governor. (She was twenty-eight and the election code said the governor had to be at least thirty-two years old.) The FBI tried to get this fact reported in the media in an attempt to discredit the campaign.

The FBI looked at participation of young people in politics

differently from the way the SWP did. The FBI wanted young people out; the SWP welcomed them. After all, it was mainly young people who were the leaders of the movements to change American society for the better—and those leaders should serve in public office, the SWP thought. Running a young person, especially a young antiwar leader like Judy White, helped dramatize the discrimination against young people in the electoral process. You couldn't vote until you were twenty-one. (The constitutional amendment lowering the voting age to eighteen wasn't ratified until July 1971.) But you had to live with the policies—and wars—determined by older people.

Should an "underage" candidate be elected, it would not be too difficult for the voters to make sure their chosen candidate took office. For one thing, a constitutional amendment lowering the age requirement could be passed.

But the FBI wasn't interested in leaving such questions of politics to the American public. According to the documents, the bureau wanted to try to discredit Judy White and had decided to rely on the *Daily News* to do the job for them, but the New York City CBS television affiliate did it instead. A copy of the transcript of the editorial broadcast by the station immediately following the election is reproduced in the files.

White recently read the Cointelpro papers relating to her campaign. "It was the CBS editorial that started the whole controversy that led to the passage of what was called the 'Judy White law,' " she recalled.

As the documents show, the state legislature soon passed a law altering the election code to require that a candidate be old enough to assume an office in order to run for it.

"Even before the election, CBS was making effective use of the charge that I wasn't 'old enough.' I'm sure the FBI must have planted this idea," White said.

"We were getting many hours of broadcast time, which was uncommon then. But a few days before the elections it abruptly stopped.

"I was scheduled to go on CBS with the other candidates for governor on a special one-hour program. Suddenly, CBS informed us that my appearance was canceled. They said I was not a legally qualified candidate because of my age."

Of course, though White was not old enough to hold the office, she was legally qualified to run for it; that was why the law was changed. Today people under thirty are legally ineligible to run for governor of New York.

These documents indicate that the FBI may have been responsible for getting this legislation on the books.

The next set of documents concerns an FBI undercover plot implemented the previous year. The city was Denver, where the Socialist Workers party was fielding candidates in the elections for school board.

"In an effort to prevent these people from being elected," the Denver office proposed to FBI headquarters that a letter be sent to the president of the Denver school board to "alert" him to the fact that socialists were running for positions on the board.

The Denver FBI included in its proposal to Washington an article about the SWP that had appeared in the *Denver Post* the previous year. That article branded the SWP "as both subversive and on the Attorney General's list of subversive organizations." The FBI likes the media to refer to the SWP in this fashion, and there is good reason to believe that the FBI was involved in writing that story.

(The attorney general's list, a McCarthy-era compilation of "subversive" organizations, was officially abolished by Nixon during his last days in office. However, Justice Department officials say the government still maintains a secret list of fifty-two "subversive organizations" for use by government agencies.)

The FBI seemed to be irritated because the Denver press had failed to label the SWP as subversive when the party announced its school board candidates.

Washington gave the go-ahead for a letter from "a concerned mother."

The next group of documents exposes an FBI operation aimed at a Black socialist. The FBI tried to ruin Paul Boutelle's campaign for mayor of New York in 1969 and to drive him and other Blacks out of the SWP.

The FBI discovered through its surveillance of the SWP that Boutelle had been arrested in New Jersey and falsely charged with possession of stolen property while he was helping a friend to move. The FBI sought to exploit this by circulating information on the arrest to the press.

While no New York newspaper ever printed the story, the FBI indicates in a document printed here that the information might have been passed on to supporters of Mayor John Lindsay, who was running for reelection, thus encouraging them to challenge the petitions the SWP had submitted in order to obtain ballot status.

The board of elections used this challenge as a pretext to

find some of the SWP's signatures "invalid" on some technicalities, such as the signers abbreviating words in their addresses, or writing in incorrect ward and precinct numbers or, in the case of married women, using "Mrs." with their husbands' names instead of their own first names. The party was forced to run a write-in campaign. If this was caused by the FBI, as the agent in charge of Cointelpro suggests, that makes this one of the more successful Cointelpro operations.

The second part of the plot was less successful. The FBI followed up by mailing Boutelle a racist letter, purportedly from a white member of the SWP, attacking him for both the arrest and remarks Boutelle had made at an earlier SWP convention.

The effect of this letter, as recorded in FBI files and as recalled by members of the SWP who were in New York in 1969, is instructive.

Boutelle brought the letter directly to the attention of a meeting of the New York SWP, where it could be openly discussed. Party members immediately spotted the letter as the work of police. "We've been through this before," the FBI quotes one member as saying. "No one in the SWP wrote that."

* * *

There are those who are horrified by the Watergate crimes, yet feel that the use of the same tactics against socialists is excusable in the name of "national security." They accept the notion that certain ideas and the advocates of those ideas are beyond the pale.

One of the main lessons of both Watergate and the Cointelpro papers is that the use of such illegal methods against political opponents cannot remain limited to socialists. If tolerated, they will inevitably be aimed at other forces in this society who run into conflict with the powers that be.

Memorandum

TO : DIRECTOR, FBI (████)   DATE: November 2, 1961

FROM : SAC, DETROIT (████)

SUBJECT: SOCIALIST WORKERS PARTY
INTERNAL SECURITY - SWP
DISRUPTION PROGRAM

Re Bureau letter to New York, October 12, 1961,
captioned as above.

The following are suggestions regarding initiating
a Socialist Workers Party (SWP) Disruption Program on a
limited basis:

1. Referenced Bureau letter states the SWP has,
over the past several years, been openly espousing its line
on a local and national basis through running candidates for
public office. Letters to newspaper editors and other various
columns in newspapers publishing letters from subscribers
could be mailed to newspapers, signed by fictitious names,
and pointing out that at the same time these individuals are
candidates for political office in the United States they are
members of the SWP, an organization dedicated to the revolutionary overthrow of the United States Government. The fact that
they are SWP candidates indicates that they are SWP members.
Information from public sources could be pooled from all
offices indicating the anarchist and revolutionary basis of the
SWP. The fact that the SWP has been cited by the Attorney
General of the United States as a subversive organization could
be fully outlined. This fact is probably not as generally known
as it should be. This procedure would alert the public to the
fact that in voting for a SWP candidate they are not voting for
an innocuous "Socialist" candidate or a "labor" candidate but
for a candidate dedicated to the overthrow of the United States
Government.

The above idea of labeling the SWP as a subversive
organization which it is, could be expanded upon and other
means of adequately publishing this fact utilized. Leaflets
outlining the above could be mimeographed and surreptitiously

Pages 46 and 47: Initial suggestions for disruption tactics
against the SWP submitted by the Detroit office in November 1961, less than a month after Hoover's directive

left at polling places. The information could be forwarded
to newspaper reporters, radio and television stations, always
taking necessary precautions so that the identity of the FBI
as the source would not be disclosed.

2. With regard to the SWP supporting causes such
as CASTRO'S Cuba and groups concerned with integration
problems in the south, it is known that the SWP to a certain
extent dominates the Fair Play for Cuba Committee, is
attempting to dominate and control the Committee to Aid the
Monroe Defendants and is seeking sponsors for this latter
organization. The following ideas ▓▓▓▓▓▓▓▓▓▓▓▓▓▓▓
▓▓▓▓▓▓▓▓▓▓▓▓▓▓▓▓▓▓▓▓▓▓▓▓ could be utilized:

a. Letters could be mailed to the sponsors of such
organizations outlining the subversive connections of the
officers of the organizations and advising them as to the nature
of the organization that they are sponsoring. This might cause
sponsors to publicly withdraw their support.

b. When organizations such as above rent halls for
meetings and so forth, information regarding the real nature
of the organization and the subversive connections of its
leaders could by various means be channeled to the management
of the halls so that they will refuse to rent the hall to the
organization. This could be repeated causing the disruption
of proposed meetings.

c. Reporters, newspapers and other media could be
informed regarding the subversive affiliations of the leaders
of these organizations with the hope that they will publicize
this information (for example ED SHAW, Midwest Regional Director
of the Fair Play for Cuba Committee is a SWP member).

Locally the Detroit Office will use the ideas and
methods ▓▓▓▓▓▓▓▓▓▓▓▓▓▓▓▓▓▓▓▓▓▓▓▓▓▓▓▓▓▓▓▓▓▓
▓▓▓▓▓▓ fitted to and implemented by ideas and methods appropriate
for the limited SWP membership. However, prior Bureau approval
will be obtained by any new counter-intelligence operations.
FOR

*launching the program. The proposals center on the use of
the "subversive" label to smear the party and any causes it
was supporting.*

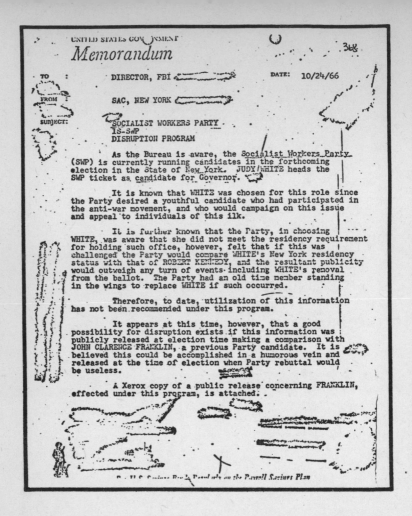

UNITED STATES GOVERNMENT

Memorandum

TO : DIRECTOR, FBI   DATE: 10/24/66

FROM : SAC, NEW YORK

SUBJECT: SOCIALIST WORKERS PARTY
IS-SWP
DISRUPTION PROGRAM

    As the Bureau is aware, the Socialist Workers Party (SWP) is currently running candidates in the forthcoming election in the State of New York. JUDY WHITE heads the SWP ticket as candidate for Governor.

    It is known that WHITE was chosen for this role since the Party desired a youthful candidate who had participated in the anti-war movement, and who would campaign on this issue and appeal to individuals of this ilk.

    It is further known that the Party, in choosing WHITE, was aware that she did not meet the residency requirement for holding such office, however, felt that if this was challenged the Party would compare WHITE's New York residency status with that of ROBERT KENNEDY, and the resultant publicity would outweigh any turn of events including WHITE's removal from the ballot. The Party had an old time member standing in the wings to replace WHITE if such occurred.

    Therefore, to date, utilization of this information has not been recommended under this program.

    It appears at this time, however, that a good possibility for disruption exists if this information was publicly released at election time making a comparison with JOHN CLARENCE FRANKLIN, a previous Party candidate. It is believed this could be accomplished in a humorous vein and released at the time of election when Party rebuttal would be useless.

    A Xerox copy of a public release concerning FRANKLIN, effected under this program, is attached.

Pages 48–51: In 1966, the FBI attempted to undermine Judy White's campaign for governor of New York by getting the press to publicize the fact that if elected she would not meet the age requirement for holding that office. In the memo on page 51 the bureau takes credit for helping in-

The following example is submitted for the Bureau's consideration in furnishing this information to the friendly writer of the NYC newspaper which previously published the attached article:

"HER SLIP IS SHOWING...

Proud of my reputation as an independent thinker, I may once again hop, skip and jump over the voting machine. My choice for Governor, as leader of the ticket, should reflect the utmost consideration as to which candidate will do the best job. The choice, however, is made a little easier by the presence on the ballot of JUDY WHITE, candidate for Governor on the ticket of the Socialist Workers Party. JUDY's platform indicates that, if elected, she will crusade for a voting age of 18; however, her own age of 28 would preclude her serving, even if elected. Seems there are only three requirements for this job in the State Constitution, to wit: a U.S. citizen, attainment of 30 years of age, residency in New York for five years immediately preceding election. Her residency in New York for less than six months also appears to leave something to be desired. The Socialist Workers Party seems to have a flair for running curious candidates as evidenced by JOHN CLARENCE FRANKLIN, its 1961 candidate for president of the borough of Manhattan. JOHN's arrest record ran from petty larceny to first degree murder and later received free room and board in Clinton Prison. How such candidates manage a spot on the ballot is interesting speculation. Do you get the impression its leg-pulling time?"

The NYO feels that publication of the above information, in the manner recommended, would seriously and effectively embarrass the SWP. It would, furthermore, spotlight another example of the Party's ineptness and lack of serious-mindedness in its efforts to influence others. It is, therefore, felt that this latest exposure could result in another "nail in the coffin" of the Party in the eyes of other radical groups, together with unaffiliated individuals who might be swayed by the Party line.

spire the "Judy White law" barring young people from the ballot. The reference to John Clarence Franklin on page 48 concerns an earlier FBI operation against a Black socialist candidate, which is described in chapter 4.

Editorial/©2

WCBS-TV, 51 WEST 52 STREET, NEW YORK, N.Y. 10019

WCBS-TV Editorials express the views of the station's management on important community issues. Because opinions on these issues may differ, WCBS-TV will consider requests for time on the station from those representing differing views. CLARK B. GEORGE, Vice President, CBS Television Stations Division and General Manager, WCBS-TV.

SUBJECT: ELECTION LAW REFORM

SPONSOR: Michael F. Keating

BROADCAST: November 18, 1966
              6 PM Evening Report
              November 21, 1966
              7 AM Morning Report

In covering the recent elections in New York, we discovered what we consider to be a serious flaw in our election law, a flaw that should be corrected immediately. And the flaw is that, under the present system, a person can run for governor or other state offices even though that person may not be eligible to serve if elected, according to the provisions of our state Constitution.

For example, the state Constitution says that in order to serve as governor, a person must be 30 years old, a resident of the state for the five years preceding the election, and a United States citizen. But, the Secretary of State tells us, there is no procedure that calls for an automatic check to determine that a candidate nominated for governor meets those qualifications.

Now, in the past election, the Socialist Worker Party candidate for governor was a woman named Judith White. But if she had been elected, according to the Constitution she could not have served, because she is 28 years old. And, as I mentioned, the state Constitution says that the governor must be at least 30.

Since the Constitution does contain certain qualifications for the office of governor, then the same qualifications should apply to the people who run for that office. It doesn't make sense to have a candidate running for an office that the Constitution says he is not eligible to fill. Everyone who votes for that candidate throws his vote away, and, in a tight race, those votes could be crucial. If that candidate should happen to win election, it could result in a breakdown of our government.

In our opinion, the law should ensure that candidates on the ballot are eligible to serve in the office for which they are running.

* * *

We would like to remind our viewers that WCBS-TV will consider requests for time for the presentation of views differing from those expressed in our editorials.

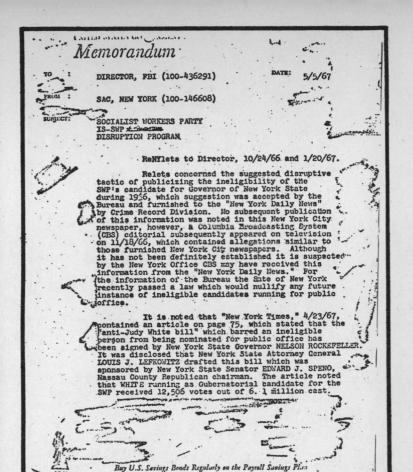

United States Government

Memorandum

ReNYlets to Director, 10/24/66 and 1/20/67.

Relets concerned the suggested disruptive tactic of publicizing the ineligibility of the SWP's candidate for Governor of New York State during 1956, which suggestion was accepted by the Bureau and furnished to the "New York Daily News" by Crime Record Division. No subsequent publication of this information was noted in this New York City newspaper, however, a Columbia Broadcasting System (CBS) editorial subsequently appeared on television on 11/18/66, which contained allegations similar to those furnished New York City newspapers. Although it has not been definitely established it is suspected by the New York Office CBS may have received this information from the "New York Daily News." For the information of the Bureau the State of New York recently passed a law which would nullify any future instance of ineligible candidates running for public office.

It is noted that "New York Times," 4/23/67, contained an article on page 75, which stated that the "anti-Judy White bill" which barred an ineligible person from being nominated for public office has been signed by New York State Governor NELSON ROCKEFELLER. It was disclosed that New York State Attorney General LOUIS J. LEFKOWITZ drafted this bill which was sponsored by New York State Senator EDWARD J. SPENO, Nassau County Republican chairman. The article noted that WHITE running as Gubernatorial candidate for the SWP received 12,506 votes out of 6.1 million cast.

51

FBI

Date: 5/4/65

Transmit the following

Via   AIRTEL

TO: DIRECTOR, FBI

FROM: SAC, DENVER

SUBJECT: COMMUNIST PARTY, USA
           COUNTERINTELLIGENCE PROGRAM
           INTERNAL SECURITY - C
           (SOCIALIST WORKERS PARTY)

Re Denver letter 4/20/65 and Bureau letter 4/28/65 captioned as above.

Enclosed for the Bureau is one copy each of articles appearing in the 4/25/65 issue of the "Denver Post" and 5/4/65 issue of the "Rocky Mountain News" concerning upcoming Denver school board election.

Referenced Denver letter contained information that ALLEN TAPLIN, Branch Organizer of the Denver Branch, SWP, was running for the Denver School Board, which election is being held 5/18/65. However, BARBARA TAPLIN and HOWARD WALLACE, both members of the Denver Branch, SWP, have filed their candidacy for election to the school board instead of ALLEN TAPLIN as previously reported.

Bureau authority is requested prior to 5/11/65 for Denver to send the revised suggested letter and enclosed newspaper clippings to the President of the Denver School Board in an effort to prevent these people from being elected.

The suggested letter is as follows:

Pages 52 and 53: In 1965 the Denver office of the FBI outlined a scheme to send a fake letter from a "concerned mother" giving ammunition for red-baiting of a socialist

"Dear Sir:

"Recently while discussing with a friend the various candidates for the upcoming Denver School Board Election, I observed the names of Mrs. Barbara Taplin, 1631 Pearl Street, and Howard Wallace, 1860 Race Street, Denver, Colorado as candidates for the Denver School Board with their political parties listed as SWP.

"I vividly recall that Mr. Allen Taplin who is listed in the 'Post' article dated 4/25/65 as the husband of Mrs. Barbara Taplin, as the unsuccessful Socialist Workers Party candidate for the United States House of Representatives in 1964. In an article of the 'Denver Post' which I am enclosing for your information, this organization is listed as both subversive and on the Attorney General's list of subversive organizations. The article also hints that Mr. Taplin is a communist.

"Being a conscientious voter and mother of school age children, I feel that someone should do something to prevent persons of this sort from being elected to the school board.

"Although I am much in favor of publicly opposing these people, I feel it best for my family's sake that I withhold my name and leave this situation in your capable hands.

"A Concerned Mother"

If authority is granted to mail this letter, Bureau instructions concerning previous approved letter will be followed.

school board candidate. The aim is clearly stated: "to prevent these people from being elected." Washington approved the operation.

of the SWP signatures were invalid. According to the "Daily
News", because the SWP had filed before LINDSAY's Independent
Party, it won a top-line position on the ballot. Thus LINDSAY,
the Liberal Party nominee, by challenging the SWP petition
was making "a bid to win a second top line on the Nov. 4 ballot".

On 9/19/69, "The New York Times" reported tnat, "The
Socialist Workers Party was removed yesterday from the ballot
in the city-wide November elections when the Board of Elections
ruled that most of the signatures on its petition were invalid"
.... and this action "virtually assured Mayor LINDSAY a second
top spot on the voting machines for his Independent Party".

It is not known to what extent the information regarding BOUTELLE's arrest, if known to LINDSAY supporters, encouraged
them to challenge the SWP petition. In any event, the SWP
political campaign has been disrupted in New York.

In an effort to further polarize blacks and whites
within the SWP, and particularly to further irritate BOUTELLE
over the "racism" within the Party, Bureau authority is requested
to prepare the following anonymous letter on commercial stationery
for transmittal to BOUTELLE at his home address, 2159 Davidson
Ave., Bronx, NY:

    "'Comrade' Paul"

        "Some of us within the Party are fed up with
    the subversive effect you are having on the Party,
    but since a few see your presence as an asset
    (because of your color only) not much can be said
    openly.

        "Your racist remarks at the Convention show
    you to be utterly useless to the revolution to come.
    And then, as could have been expected, you and your
    friends have put the Party in a position of possibly
    having to defend a common thief.

        "Why don't you and the rest of your fellow
    party monkeys hook up with the Panthers where you'd
    feel at home?

Pages 54–56: *The New York FBI office was unsuccessful
in its efforts to publicize the fact that Paul Boutelle had
been arrested on trumped-up charges, but claimed part of
the credit for getting him ruled off the ballot in the 1969
New York mayoral election. Washington approved New*

"Maybe then we could get on with the job Trotsky had in mind for us.

"Your 'nasty' friends".

Since confidential sources feel that BOUTELLE is merely being "used" because of his color, and his Convention remarks indicate he might be aware of this fact, it is expected that BOUTELLE may become more outspoken regarding racism within the Party, all of which would create some diversion within its ranks, and could result in BOUTELLE's resignation and conceivably other Negroes with whom BOUTELLE is friendly.

If authority is granted to prepare and mail the above letter, all precautions will be taken to insure the mailing cannot be associated with the FBI.

York's proposal to send a racist letter, ostensibly from a white member, to "polarize blacks and whites within the SWP" and demoralize Boutelle. The reason for the operation (page 56) is the bureau's complaint that the party is "growing rapidly" and running candidates for office.

SAC, New York ~~~~~~~~~   10/8/69

Director, FBI ~~~~~~~~~

SOCIALIST WORKERS PARTY - DISRUPTION PROGRAM
IS - SWP

     Reurlet 9/30/69.

     Authority granted to prepare and mail anonymous
letter set forth in relet.

     Insure usual precaution taken in order that the
letter cannot be traced back to the Bureau. Advise the
Bureau of the results.

NOTE:

     The Socialist Workers Party (SWP) is a militant
communist splinter organization which is growing rapidly.
Members of the SWP are running for the office of mayor in
New York City and Atlanta, Georgia. Candidate for mayor of
New York City is Paul Boutelle, who is a Negro and who is a
national leader of the SWP. At the SWP National Convention
in August, 1969, Boutelle criticized "racism" existing in the
SWP. NYO proposes to exploit this issue by sending an anonymous
letter to Boutelle in the expectation that Boutelle, who is
quick tempered, will become even more outspoken on this issue.
This will thus create a devisive split within the SWP. Such
action may well result in Boutelle's resignation from the SWP
along with other members who support him, thus crippling the
SWP in its march for expansion. The proposed letter starts on
page three of the attached incoming communication.

2 Inciting violence: "It should be an interesting experience for Mr. Halstead"

Early in 1946 a young sailor named Fred Halstead was stationed on a ship off the coast of China. World War II had just ended, but on the mainland of China the fighting had not stopped. A civil war was raging.

Back in Washington the rulers of this country were very interested in the outcome of that struggle. They would have liked to send their army in to back up Chiang Kai-shek's crumbling forces, but their attempts to stall the demobilization of American troops after the war provoked massive protests among the GIs. It was clear that large-scale U.S. military intervention in China was out of the question.

Two decades later when the United States began committing thousands of troops to another Asian country in an attempt to hold back a revolution, Fred Halstead remembered what he had seen while he was in the navy. He was convinced that there were important lessons for the growing movement against the war in Vietnam.

In an interview, Halstead talked about this and about some revelations contained in the Cointelpro papers. Halstead was the Socialist Workers party candidate for president in 1968. During the campaign he made a trip to Vietnam. It now turns out the FBI had tried to sabotage that trip.

Among the documents turned over to the SWP under federal court order is evidence that the FBI wrote a "news story" that it sought to have placed in the military press.

The FBI's purpose was to provoke violence against the socialist presidential candidate during his visit to Vietnam. "It should be an interesting experience for Mr. HALSTEAD when he encounters the men who have served both their own country and others in the interest of freedom," the FBI's article concluded.

Before discussing that experience, Halstead described what he had seen at the close of the Second World War.

"I was attached to a ship that was part of the Seventh Fleet in Chinese waters. Ostensibly, we were there to repatriate Japanese troops," Halstead said.

"But after unloading our passengers in Japan, we found ourselves loading up again. This time with Chinese troops, which we took up to a port in northern China. This was part of the use of the American navy to assist Chiang's offensive in the Chinese civil war.

"Well, most of us didn't know there was such a thing as a civil war in China until we found ourselves more or less involved in it."

The GIs had just finished one war, and they didn't like the idea of getting into another one. Soon a protest movement developed.

"I remember walking into the Red Cross building in Shanghai where GIs would go to get coffee and hamburgers," Halstead said. "There I saw this big banner with the words: 'GIs unite! We want to go home!'"

There were mimeograph machines aboard the ships and on the army posts, and leaflets expressing that demand were reproduced. "I didn't organize all this, but I picked up leaflets and passed them out," Halstead recalled.

He also remembers attending meetings where some of the organizers gave speeches condemning imperialism. "But mainly, it was a movement of GIs who just wanted to go home."

They held some big demonstrations. There was one in Manila and another in Shanghai. The message got through, and orders soon came in to return to the United States.

"This made an impression on me that I didn't forget. That you could organize among GIs," Halstead remarked. "Just that simple proposition."

When he got back home, Halstead had some additional experiences that he later found useful in the antiwar movement. He went to work as a civilian seaman in the merchant marine, where he was a member of the Sailors' Union of the Pacific. But before long he was "screened" off that job by the Coast Guard for being a "subversive."

"A fellow named John Mahoney up in Seattle had been fired

for criticizing the bureaucracy of the union," Halstead recalled. "A lot of people who had come to his defense were fired. I had passed out some leaflets on the case. That's probably the reason my name got turned over to the Coast Guard."

After going to school on the GI Bill for a while, Halstead got a job as an automobile worker and became active in a United Auto Workers (UAW) organizing drive.

"The Korean War came along and we lost that drive, in part because of the hysteria around the war and the red-baiting that developed."

Halstead next learned garment cutting, which has been his trade ever since. As a member of the International Ladies' Garment Workers' Union (ILGWU), he participated in the union's organizing campaigns. At times, Halstead was assigned by the union to get a job in an unorganized shop. The ILGWU paid him the difference between the salary he received there and union-scale wages, while he spearheaded the drive for union recognition.

Halstead also participated in efforts during that period to organize agricultural workers in California.

In 1953 Halstead moved to Detroit, where he landed a job in an automobile plant cutting cloth for the upholstery in cars.

"I had been working there for about a year when the Square D strike broke out," Halstead said. That strike occurred during the depths of the witch-hunt and was of some importance.

Square D was an electrical manufacturing firm under contract to the United Electrical Workers, which was one of the unions expelled from the CIO for "Communist domination." The company was out to break the strike and was nearly successful.

What finally saved the union was the massive response of UAW militants, including Fred Halstead, who rallied to the defense of the Square D strikers and beat back the company and the scab-herding cops. In the course of the strike, Halstead became the victim of a frame-up attempt by the Detroit police and their "loyalty" squad. But the cops' red-scare hoax failed, and the charges were eventually dropped.

When the movement against United States involvement in Vietnam began to develop, Halstead became one of its leaders. He joined the staff of the New York Fifth Avenue Vietnam Peace Parade Committee upon its inception in 1965, and he remained there until he left to run for president in 1967. After his campaign, he again worked in the antiwar movement, and he was involved in organizing every major national demonstration.

Today, after years of antiwar demonstrations by veterans and frequent manifestations of antiwar sentiment within the military, it may seem hard to believe that at first many opponents of the war wrote off GIs as "war criminals" and rejected the possibility of winning them as allies. But that was all too frequently the case.

"When the antiwar movement came along, there were discussions about where we should spread the word," Halstead recalled. "One obvious place, I would suggest, was right inside the army.

" 'You're crazy,' people would say to me. 'They are butchers, and there is nothing we can do about that.'

"I would tell them that they were wrong, that GIs are just ordinary people who will be responsive to the same arguments as civilians," Halstead continued.

"I knew GIs could be reached because I had been a GI myself and I had seen GIs organize."

The Trip to Vietnam

Why did Halstead decide to visit Vietnam in the summer of 1968? During the presidential campaign that year Lyndon Johnson tried to convey the impression that the war was almost over. Nixon and Humphrey, the candidates of the two capitalist parties, made a pact between themselves not to make the war an issue in the campaign.

The SWP's candidate went to Vietnam as part of the socialist strategy to try to inject the war into the presidential campaign as *the* major issue.

"We demanded the immediate withdrawal of the American forces as the only way to end the killing over there and as the only legal and moral thing for the United States to do," Halstead recalled.

"That year there was a tendency on the part of some in the antiwar movement to get into electoral activity as a *substitute* for antiwar demonstrations. Through this campaign we encouraged the antiwar movement to stay in the streets."

There was another reason for making the trip. "We wanted to illustrate to the antiwar movement that it could reach GIs," Halstead said, "and we wanted to demonstrate to the GIs that the antiwar movement was on their side."

On August 15, 1968, Fred Halstead arrived in Saigon. He was accompanied by Barry Sheppard, who was at that time editor of the *Militant,* a socialist newsweekly. They spent five days in

Vietnam, including a visit to the big army base at Long Binh, talking with GIs. The *Militant* carried reports from Vietnam on what they found.

"We were interested in talking to the American GIs who were on the scene," Halstead said. "They had a right to vote and to listen to what the candidates had to say. They also had a right to have an opinion on the war—a greater right than any American citizen, including the president. I went there to ask them what that opinion was."

What did he find? "The overwhelming majority of them were not willing to suddenly join the peace movement, but they weren't supporters of the war either," Halstead remembered.

They were mainly confused, looking for answers, still making up their minds. "That was all the more reason for the antiwar movement to have the stance and attitude that they were interested in reaching GIs—were on their side," Halstead observed.

Barry Sheppard also gave his impressions. "We found no hostility to us among any troops," he recalled, "including those who were for the war at that point."

"There were some antiwar figures who thought I would get into trouble talking to GIs in Vietnam," Halstead remembered. "And I might have gotten into some difficulty speaking to the GIs the way they did. If I had called them butchers and told them they were immoral for not refusing the draft, I probably would have gotten a fist in my face."

Instead, Halstead explained that he was a candidate from the United States who was active in the antiwar movement. He said that he thought this country never belonged in Vietnam and should get out immediately.

"I was received in a courteous and sometimes friendly way," Halstead remembered. "Never in a hostile way."

Is there any evidence that the FBI was successful in its goal of getting their story about Halstead into the military press in order to provoke an attack? The item was never picked up and printed as far as Halstead knows.

"The response we found among the soldiers in Vietnam is the key to understanding why this particular project failed," Sheppard observed. "Even those who supported the war offered no strong political motivation. They would argue along the lines that since so many lives had already been lost, the war should continue so that those deaths would not have been in vain. An appeal to anticommunism wasn't put forward as a compelling reason to stay in Vietnam."

However, Sheppard and Halstead both remembered something, which in retrospect they feel might have been a setup under FBI influence.

Among the best places to meet and talk with GIs, they found, were the bars. One day the two socialists were sitting on stools at a bar, when a white sailor sat down beside Sheppard and began talking. While Fred was carrying on a conversation with a group of Black GIs on the other side, the white sailor made a remark about "Black power niggers." It was clearly audible to the Black soldiers.

A Black GI immediately reached over and smashed the sailor in the face. There rapidly ensued a fist fight, which Halstead and Sheppard managed to avoid. Fortunately, the automatic rifles which some of the GIs in the bar were carrying did not come into play.

Halstead and Sheppard suspect that the white sailor could have been acting under instructions to start a fight in hopes that the two socialists would become caught up—or even seriously injured—in a fight between Black and white GIs. On the other hand, they think it could have been, as Halstead put it, "just a little piece of America."

The antiwar movement as a whole would soon be convinced of the possibility of reaching GIs. "What really changed their mind was that they saw with their own eyes the GIs turning against the war," Halstead told me. "You couldn't draft 30,000 youth a month in 1968 and 1969 without getting a lot who had been involved in the antiwar movement in one way or another. Then it just spread all over the army."

The interview with Halstead took place in April 1975. The Saigon army was collapsing and the revolutionary forces were sweeping through Vietnam. By drastically limiting Washington's ability to use its military forces in China, the movement Halstead had seen almost thirty years before when he was a GI in the Pacific had been instrumental in the victory of the Chinese Revolution.

Did he see any parallels with Vietnam? "I think the fact that the United States finds it so difficult to put its military forces back into Vietnam is a very important factor in the victories that the liberation forces have won.

"The Pentagon keeps moaning that their hands are tied. Well, what tied their hands is the American antiwar movement."

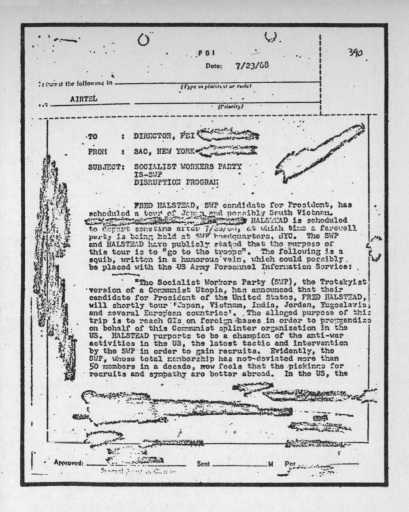

FBI

Date: 7/23/68

Transmit the following in _____
(Type in plaintext or code)

AIRTEL _____
(Priority)

TO : DIRECTOR, FBI

FROM : SAC, NEW YORK

SUBJECT: SOCIALIST WORKERS PARTY
IS-SWP
DISRUPTION PROGRAM

FRED HALSTEAD, SWP candidate for President, has
scheduled a tour of Japan and possibly South Vietnam.
HALSTEAD is scheduled
to depart sometime after 7/25/68, at which time a farewell
party is being held at SWP headquarters, NYC. The SWP
and HALSTEAD have publicly stated that the purpose of
this tour is to "go to the troops". The following is a
squib, written in a humorous vein, which could possibly
be placed with the US Army Personnel Information Service:

"The Socialist Workers Party (SWP), the Trotskyist
version of a Communist Utopia, has announced that their
candidate for President of the United States, FRED HALSTEAD,
will shortly tour 'Japan, Vietnam, India, Jordan, Yugoslavia,
and several European countries'. The alleged purpose of this
trip is to reach GIs on foreign bases in order to propagandize
on behalf of this Communist splinter organization in the
US. HALSTEAD purports to be a champion of the anti-war
activities in the US, the latest tactic and intervention
by the SWP in order to gain recruits. Evidently, the
SWP, whose total membership has not deviated more than
50 members in a decade, now feels that the pickings for
recruits and sympathy are better abroad. In the US, the

Approved: _____ Sent _____ M Per _____

Pages 63–66: *FBI memos proposing to disrupt Fred Halstead's 1968 visit to Vietnam to talk to GIs. The tactic is the familiar one of planting red-baiting information in the press—in this case the armed forces press, using military intelligence channels. This operation had one additional special feature: the FBI "news" item ends with a thinly veiled invitation to GIs to assault the antiwar leader.*

"SWP has recently suffered its usual reversal among fellow radical organizations in its attempts to infiltrate and dominate the anti-war scene. HALSTEAD is scheduled to push for the return of all US personnel abroad. As a past champion of FIDEL CASTRO, he believes all countries should be left to fend for themselves and establish their future Utopias on the scale of the current Cuban Paradise. Intervention into the affairs of nations by countries or forces other than "the imperialist US" is not a plank in HALSTEAD's platform. It should be an interesting experience for Mr. HALSTEAD when he encounters the men who have served both their own country and others in the interest of freedom".

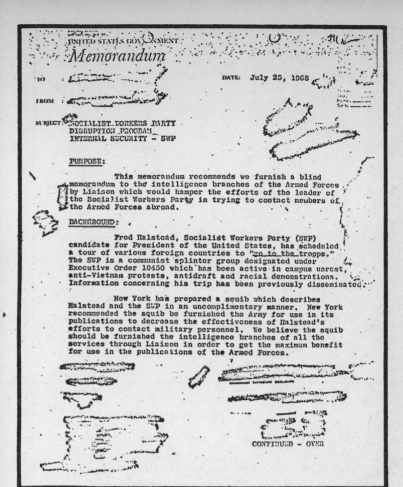

UNITED STATES GOVERNMENT

Memorandum

TO :

DATE: July 25, 1968

FROM :

SUBJECT: SOCIALIST WORKERS PARTY
DISRUPTION PROGRAM
INTERNAL SECURITY - SWP

PURPOSE:

This memorandum recommends we furnish a blind memorandum to the intelligence branches of the Armed Forces by Liaison which would hamper the efforts of the leader of the Socialist Workers Party in trying to contact members of the Armed Forces abroad.

BACKGROUND:

Fred Halstead, Socialist Workers Party (SWP) candidate for President of the United States, has scheduled a tour of various foreign countries to "go to the troops." The SWP is a communist splinter group designated under Executive Order 10450 which has been active in campus unrest, anti-Vietnam protests, antidraft and racial demonstrations. Information concerning his trip has been previously disseminated.

New York has prepared a squib which describes Halstead and the SWP in an uncomplimentary manner. New York recommended the squib be furnished the Army for use in its publications to decrease the effectiveness of Halstead's efforts to contact military personnel. We believe the squib should be furnished the intelligence branches of all the services through Liaison in order to get the maximum benefit for use in the publications of the Armed Forces.

CONTINUED - OVER

65

The proposed squib is attached in blind memorandum form. It does not jeopardize any sources.

RECOMMENDATION:

It is recommended the squib be approved and sent by Liaison to the intelligence branches of the Armed Forces.

3 Targeting a Black candidate: "Determine if there is anything derogatory in his background"

"A review is being conducted of CLIFTON DE BERRY's file to determine if there is anything derogatory in his background which might cause embarrassment to the SWP if publicly exposed."

Those words appear in a secret FBI memorandum dated October 17, 1963. Of the nearly 1,200 pages of Cointelpro files released thus far in response to the SWP suit, more concern Clifton DeBerry than any other single individual. In 1964 DeBerry became the first Black person ever to run for president of the United States when he was nominated by the SWP.

Why was the FBI so interested in DeBerry? What was it about this man and his political activities that caused the FBI to devote so much energy to trying to discredit him?

In an interview, DeBerry talked about his background—his many years of activity in the union movement and the Black liberation struggle.

DeBerry was born in Holly Springs, Mississippi. His family sent him at a young age to live with relatives in Chicago, where they hoped he would find more opportunities open to him.

Instinctively a rebel, DeBerry was becoming involved in "the gang-war scene and about to get into trouble." Fortunately, he ran into a friend who persuaded him to go down South and take part in some union organizing efforts.

In late 1942 the two went to Louisiana, where they organized textile workers. "Then we went to a little town just outside Nashville [Tennessee] and organized a John Deere farm equipment plant there," DeBerry recalled.

After returning to Chicago and participating in several different union organizing drives, DeBerry landed a job at the big International Harvester plant.

"They started me off in the shipping department at seventy-seven cents an hour. Our job classification was 'laborer,'" De-Berry remembered. "I had a talk with the grievance committee representative about changing the wording. We organized the guys and went out on strike for a couple of hours after lunch."

They won. Along with the classification change came a pay boost up to $1.35 an hour. "After that the guys there wanted to make me shop steward. But they already had one—an old-timer, who I later learned was in the Communist party.

"But since the workers were determined to make me their shop steward, some people from the CP contacted me. They told me I had to join the CP to become a shop steward. That's how I came to join the Communist party."

After the war, a strike wave swept the country. The FBI's investigation of DeBerry's background discovered that "labor trouble" charges were placed on his record during this period. How did this happen?

"We were organized at this time by a very dynamic leader, who later became president of the local. He saw the strikes coming and inspired a lot of us young guys to get prepared.

"We all went out to an old automobile junk yard. There we practiced until we had developed a technique for 'dumping' cars. That means turning them over. In anticipation of possible attempts by scabs to cross the picket lines in their cars, we constituted roving picket squads of five or six each."

The American working class was in a combative mood. They won some healthy wage increases from the corporations, most of which were in a position to grant them because of their huge war profits.

DeBerry soon became well known to the Chicago police "labor squad." They developed the habit of picking up DeBerry and his friends as soon as they appeared on the scene of a strike. The cops would take them to the station but would soon release them without pressing charges, thus effectively preventing them from performing their scab-removal operation. "That is the reason so little shows up on my record," DeBerry commented.

As always during a workers' upsurge, the creativity and ingenuity of the rank and file came to the fore, and DeBerry gave an example.

"There was this group of three women who also traveled from

picket line to picket line. They had devised a method of disabling scab drivers by throwing an air-raid warden's helmet at the windshield of the car. The driver would instinctively throw his hands up to protect his face. At that point we would move in and dump the car.

"One day a big battle was shaping up at Jones Foundry. My squad showed up early in the morning. Right away we got picked up by the cops and taken downtown. They soon released us, and we headed straight back to Jones.

"We met up with those three women and were getting ready to dump some cars, when the cops nabbed us all. They threw us into the back of one of those big, square-back paddy wagons and proceeded to take us to the station.

"Now, these women had been arrested so many times that they had developed this special trick. They would station one person at the front of the wagon to look through a tiny peephole in order to see where the vehicle was headed.

"As the cops began to steer into a left turn, the one at the peephole would signal to the others—who were sitting on benches on either side of the wagon—to prepare to stand up and move to the right. If they did this during the turn, it would flip the paddy wagon over. Another person stationed by the door would kick it just as the vehicle hit the ground. This would automatically knock the doors open, so the passengers could escape.

"So, we followed their instructions. It worked, and we headed straight back to the picket line.

"Of course, they came looking for us. They picked us up again, took us back downtown, and booked us this time," DeBerry said. "That explains how I got those charges on my record."

The Cold War

In the late 1940s the cold war began to grow more intense. The international offensive by the United States against the Soviet Union was accompanied by a domestic offensive against the labor movement, as well as against the American CP. The trade-union bureaucracy capitulated to the ruling class on both fronts.

At first the leadership of the Congress of Industrial Organizations had hesitated to endorse the new cold war foreign policy. But during the presidential elections of 1948 they backed Truman, and along with this endorsement came support of Truman's cold war policies. This was codified at the 1948 CIO convention.

The CP followed a smaller wing of the ruling class, represented by Henry Wallace and his Progressive party, which preferred a kind of détente with the Soviet Union—a continuation of the wartime cooperation.

The cutting edge of the attack on the labor movement was the Taft-Hartley Act, which had been enacted in 1947. The labor movement refused to take up a serious fight against it. Among the provisions of the new law was a prohibition on members of the CP to hold office in trade unions.

"The heads of a few of the unions, including mine [the Farm Equipment Workers], were known members of the Communist party," DeBerry said. "Philip Murray, the president of the CIO, handed them an ultimatum that they had to get rid of these CP union officials, in accordance with the provisions of Taft-Hartley, or leave the CIO."

It was at this time that DeBerry began to run into problems with the CP. Along with the president of his local, DeBerry was among those union militants who felt that the Stalinist officials were placing their own personal posts above the interests of a unified labor movement.

At the 1949 convention the CP-led unions were expelled from the CIO.

Around this time the Farm Equipment Workers merged with the United Electrical Workers, another Stalinist-controlled union. "After that, the CP took over almost everything in my local," DeBerry remembered.

"I had differences with them on a number of questions, including some of their policies during the Second World War— the no-strike pledge, civil rights, and Black caucuses."

The economic boom during the war brought unprecedented numbers of Blacks into the plants. In some factories, where they were assigned the hardest and most dangerous work, Blacks constituted a large percentage of the workers. A Black caucus movement began to emerge.

"I would discuss this caucus idea with some of the stewards in my shop and with Black leaders I knew in other locals. We decided it was a good and necessary idea in order to fight the special oppression of Blacks," DeBerry recalled.

The Black caucus movement led to the formation of the National Negro Labor Council at a convention in Cincinnati in 1950. "I was a delegate from my local. The CP was very instrumental in setting up the whole thing, but they were actually opposed to the formation of Black caucuses, although they were reluctant to come out and say it."

It was at that convention that Jean Tussey, an SWP member, sold a friend of DeBerry's a copy of the *Militant*. They liked what they read and asked if there was a chapter of the SWP in Chicago. "She said there was and gave us the names of some people to look up."

As DeBerry moved closer to the SWP and began to raise political questions with the Stalinist leadership of the Communist party, the pressure on him mounted. The CP began to bring in "specialists" who tried to persuade DeBerry politically of the errors of his ways. When that failed, the CP tried other methods.

"I ran into a couple of dudes from the neighborhood hanging around the gates in front of the plant," DeBerry recalled. "I happened to ask them what they were up to, and they told me they were there to 'educate' somebody. After a little probing I discovered they were being paid to 'educate' me.

"I convinced them that they should collect the money from the people who had put them up to this but there was no need to do the job."

Not long after this, things came to a head. There was an impending strike, which the CP was desperately trying to avert. The stewards' body voted to go out, and since the CP-controlled leadership had made no provisions for a strike, the stewards were forced to assume organizational responsibility.

But the combination of a demoralizing scandal over the CP's misuse of union funds, a House Un-American Activities Committee visit to Chicago to red-bait the union, and a well-organized strikebreaking effort led to the defeat of the strike.

"After we went back I was fired," DeBerry said. "I've always thought the CP and the company got together to get rid of me, partly because other CP members on the executive board were retained."

The country was in the grip of the McCarthyite witch-hunt, and years before the incidents documented in the Cointelpro papers, DeBerry became familiar with the way the FBI operates. "I would get a job, and it would only last three days. I would go from one job to another, and it would be the same story. The FBI would visit my boss, and I would be fired."

DeBerry finally managed to hang on to a job when a stubborn employer refused to fire him. Nonetheless, he was told that FBI agents continued to come around every three or four days to "check up" on him. DeBerry eventually became a painter, and he remains one today.

The Civil Rights Movement

In 1954 the U.S. Supreme Court handed down its historic decision on school desegregation. Soon the country would witness a new Black civil rights movement and the opening stages of a new radicalization. At this time the center of DeBerry's political activity shifted from the trade-union movement to another arena.

DeBerry was active in the Chicago chapter of the NAACP and in the Washington Park Forum, a Black community organization. In 1955, news of the lynching of Emmett Till, a Black youth from Chicago, jolted the Black community. Till was murdered by racists while visiting relatives in Mississippi. DeBerry was instrumental in organizing a mass meeting to protest the lynching.

The 1955–56 Montgomery, Alabama, boycott to end segregation on the buses signaled the beginning of the civil rights movement. In Chicago, DeBerry organized a Station Wagons to Montgomery Committee, which raised funds to purchase vehicles for use by boycotters.

DeBerry personally delivered one of the station wagons to Montgomery, where he stayed at the home of E. D. Nixon. Like DeBerry, Nixon was a veteran of the union movement who brought his organizational and political know-how to the new Black civil rights struggle. Nixon was actually the central organizer of the boycott.

"I talked with Nixon about the boycott movement, how it originated, how it functioned, and what they expected to gain," DeBerry recalled. "For the first time I met Dr. Martin Luther King, who had been persuaded to enter the fight by Nixon."

In 1960 DeBerry moved to New York. That same year a sit-in movement to desegregate public accommodations began in the South. Supporters of the desegregation fight organized a boycott of the Woolworth chain in cities outside the South in a successful attempt to bring added pressure to end segregation. DeBerry threw himself into building the Woolworth boycott in Brooklyn.

"We began to make contact with Malcolm X when he was still the main spokesman for the Nation of Islam," DeBerry said. "In late 1963 I went on a speaking tour for some informal campaigning just before I announced I was running for president. Malcolm was touring at the same time, and I would go to see him whenever I could."

It was during a tour stop in Chicago that the FBI arranged to have DeBerry arrested in order to create a scandal they hoped to use to discredit him. Just as DeBerry was about to address a socialist campaign meeting, the Chicago police stormed into the building, hauled him to the station, and booked him on charges of nonsupport of his ex-wife.

There are many censored passages throughout the Cointelpro papers, but there are *entire pages* concerning this operation that were totally blank when they were turned over to the SWP by the FBI. These blank pages obviously detailed the maneuvers the FBI engaged in to engineer DeBerry's arrest.

"One thing comes to my mind about this set-up," DeBerry said. "At the Chicago police station, I ran into a cop I knew. He had been on the labor squad during some of my earlier run-ins with the police. At one point while they were booking me, there was no one else around except the two of us. In a confidential tone he told me, 'Somebody who is high up is really interested in you.' "

The FBI followed up this episode by spending the *next two years* trying to get the news media to report both the Chicago incident and DeBerry's earlier arrests for "labor trouble." In DeBerry's case, then, the FBI interfered in two election campaigns—his 1964 race for president and his 1965 race for mayor of New York City. This intervention into the electoral process is not only illegal in itself but selective and partisan, targeting only people or parties whose ideas the FBI doesn't like. (It is worth noting that this has been applied to Democrats and Republicans as well, not just socialists. Recent disclosures prove that for years the FBI gathered damaging information about the private lives of members of Congress and major party candidates—and used that information to blackmail its "enemies" and reward its "friends.")

The 1964 Campaign

On January 7, 1964, the National Committee of the Socialist Workers party formally announced the nomination of DeBerry as the SWP's candidate for president.

Lyndon Johnson was running for reelection, and he was opposed by Barry Goldwater. Johnson campaigned as a "peace candidate" who was opposed to escalating the war, while Goldwater favored increased bombing. Most Americans took Johnson's peace rhetoric for good coin, and he won a landslide victory.

Virtually the entire left supported Johnson's candidacy. Among the most enthusiastic backers of the Democratic candidate were the members of the CP, whose attitude was summed up in the title of a pamphlet by Gus Hall: *The Eleventh Hour—Defeat The New Fascist Threat!*

The SWP and some others, in contrast, clearly nailed Johnson as the hawk he was. The historical record now shows how right they were.

In August 1964, a supposed Vietnamese attack on U.S. ships off the coast of North Vietnam provided the excuse for rushing a special resolution through Congress. It was under the authority of this Gulf of Tonkin resolution that Johnson and the subsequent presidents committed the United States to a massive military intervention in Vietnam.

DeBerry charged that the whole thing had been set up by the White House and the Pentagon. "The incidents between the U.S. destroyer and the PT boats were the pretext, not the cause, of the U.S. air attack," DeBerry said at the time. Several years later the Pentagon papers would prove that he was right.

"We of the Socialist Workers party say get all the U.S. troops, planes, and warships out of Vietnam—North and South," DeBerry demanded. "If as Johnson claims their purpose is to 'protect democracy;' then send them to Mississippi and let them do some protecting of Black Americans there."

While the FBI was secretly plotting against the Black presidential candidate, he was publicly blasting the FBI. After the disappearance of three civil rights workers slain by racists in Mississippi, DeBerry exposed the bureau's complicity.

Local cops, who were involved in the murders, had held the three in jail before they were killed. "While the three kidnapped youths were in jail in Philadelphia, Mississippi, their co-workers became fearful for their safety, and telephoned the FBI in Jackson. The FBI agent refused to help and told the rights fighters that he wouldn't have any more dealings with them," DeBerry said.

In July 1964 a group of major civil rights leaders, including Roy Wilkins and Martin Luther King, issued a call for a "moratorium" on civil rights demonstrations until after election day. The purpose was to make it easier for Johnson to hold on to the racist vote, which was threatening to go to Goldwater.

DeBerry condemned the move: "This is the surest way for

Negroes to get nothing. Black people must develop independent political force. That's the only way they can be a power and the only way they can defend themselves against the attacks of the racists which will come whether Johnson or Goldwater is elected."

When Malcolm X, who was in Egypt at the time, heard about the moratorium, he had a similar reaction. The Black leaders "have sold themselves out and become campaign managers in the Negro community for Lyndon Johnson," he charged.

During this period DeBerry's relationship with Malcolm continued to develop. "After his break with the Nation of Islam, I used to meet with him almost every Saturday when he was in the country. We would have discussions about politics—often comparing notes and checking up on what each other had been hearing about the developing nationalist response among Blacks," DeBerry recalled.

At the suggestion of Malcolm and his collaborator, James Shabazz, DeBerry spoke at a couple of classes at the Muslim Mosque, Inc., which Malcolm headed.

"We were again touring at the same time, and our paths would often criss-cross. Whenever I could I would attend his speeches. While he was too busy to make it to mine, he would send someone over," DeBerry remembered. "We had that kind of relationship."

A few months later Malcolm would be assassinated. The FBI's role in that event is a story that is yet to be told.

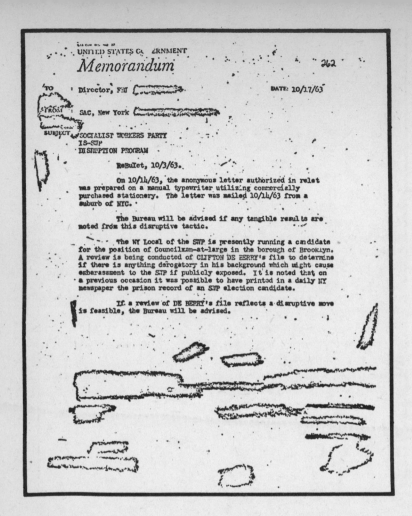

UNITED STATES GOVERNMENT

Memorandum   262

TO   : Director, FBI ⟨⟩   DATE: 10/17/63

FROM : SAC, New York ⟨⟩

SUBJECT: SOCIALIST WORKERS PARTY
         IS-SWP
         DISRUPTION PROGRAM

              ReBuLet, 10/3/63.

              On 10/14/63, the anonymous letter authorized in relet
    was prepared on a manual typewriter utilizing commercially
    purchased stationery. The letter was mailed 10/14/63 from a
    suburb of NYC.

              The Bureau will be advised if any tangible results are
    noted from this disruptive tactic.

              The NY Local of the SWP is presently running a candidate
    for the position of Councilman-at-large in the borough of Brooklyn.
    A review is being conducted of CLIFTON DE BERRY's file to determine
    if there is anything derogatory in his background which might cause
    embarassment to the SWP if publicly exposed. It is noted that on
    a previous occasion it was possible to have printed in a daily NY
    newspaper the prison record of an SWP election candidate.

              If a review of DE BERRY's file reflects a disruptive move
    is feasible, the Bureau will be advised.

While he was still running for city council in Brooklyn, the FBI's New York office targeted Clifton DeBerry for its favorite tactic against Black candidates—try to dredge up a prison or arrest record and get it sensationalized in the press.

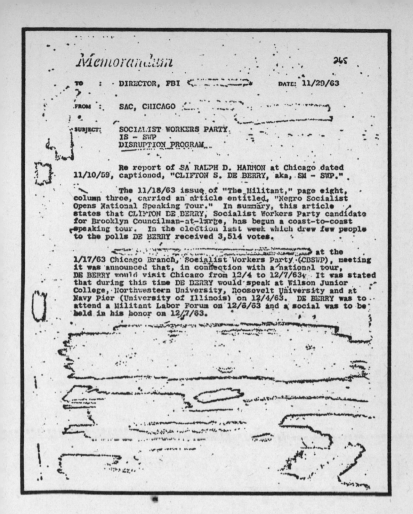

Memorandum

TO : DIRECTOR, FBI

DATE: 11/29/63

FROM : SAC, CHICAGO

SUBJECT: SOCIALIST WORKERS PARTY
IS - SWP
DISRUPTION PROGRAM

Re report of SA RALPH D. HARMON at Chicago dated 11/10/59, captioned, "CLIFTON S. DE BERRY, aka, SM - SWP."

The 11/18/63 issue of "The Militant," page eight, column three, carried an article entitled, "Negro Socialist Opens National Speaking Tour." In summary, this article states that CLIFTON DE BERRY, Socialist Workers Party candidate for Brooklyn Councilman-at-large, has begun a coast-to-coast speaking tour. In the election last week which drew few people to the polls DE BERRY received 3,514 votes.

at the 1/17/63 Chicago Branch, Socialist Workers Party (CBSWP), meeting it was announced that, in connection with a national tour, DE BERRY would visit Chicago from 12/4 to 12/7/63. It was stated that during this time DE BERRY would speak at Wilson Junior College, Northwestern University, Roosevelt University and at Navy Pier (University of Illinois) on 12/4/63. DE BERRY was to attend a Militant Labor Forum on 12/6/63 and a social was to be held in his honor on 12/7/63.

The bureau kept close track of DeBerry's activities. One reason is given in this memo: he received 3,500 votes in a local election despite low voter turnout—quite a showing for a socialist in 1964. As the accompanying essay explains, FBI interest in DeBerry dated from his days as a labor organizer.

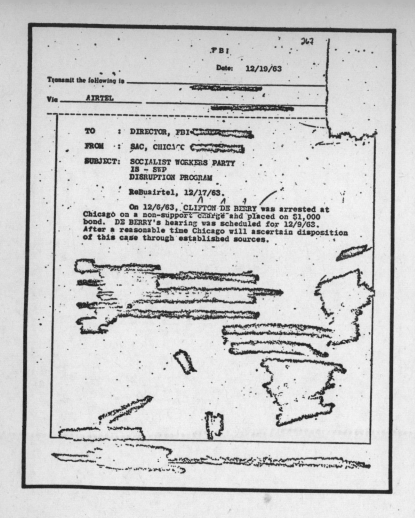

FBI

Date: 12/19/63

Transmit the following in ▓▓▓▓▓▓▓▓▓▓▓▓▓▓▓▓▓▓▓▓▓▓▓

Via   AIRTEL

TO   :   DIRECTOR, FBI▓▓▓▓▓▓▓▓

FROM :   SAC, CHICAGO ▓▓▓▓▓▓▓▓▓

SUBJECT: SOCIALIST WORKERS PARTY
               IS - SWP
               DISRUPTION PROGRAM

            ReBuairtel, 12/17/63.

          On 12/6/63, CLIFTON DE BERRY was arrested at
Chicago on a non-support charge and placed on $1,000
bond. DE BERRY's hearing was scheduled for 12/9/63.
After a reasonable time Chicago will ascertain disposition
of this case through established sources.

Chicago informs Washington that DeBerry has been
arrested on nonsupport charges—just the sort of "derogatory information" the bureau was looking for in the memo on
page 76. Several pages of the memo on page 77 were
censored; these pages may have outlined a plan to engineer
the Chicago arrest.

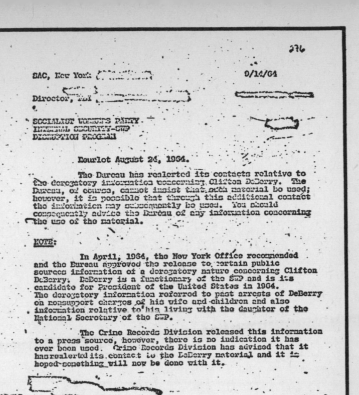

SAC, New York

9/14/64

Director, FBI

SOCIALIST WORKERS PARTY
INTERNAL SECURITY-SWP
DISRUPTION PROGRAM

Bureau let August 24, 1964.

The Bureau has realerted its contacts relative to the derogatory information concerning Clifton DeBerry. The Bureau, of course, cannot insist that such material be used; however, it is possible that through this additional contact the information may subsequently be used. You should consequently advise the Bureau of any information concerning the use of the material.

NOTE:

In April, 1964, the New York Office recommended and the Bureau approved the release to certain public sources information of a derogatory nature concerning Clifton DeBerry. DeBerry is a functionary of the SWP and is its candidate for President of the United States in 1964. The derogatory information referred to past arrests of DeBerry on nonsupport charges of his wife and children and also information relative to his living with the daughter of the National Secretary of the SWP.

The Crime Records Division released this information to a press source, however, there is no indication it has ever been used. Crime Records Division has advised that it has realerted its contact to the DeBerry material and it is hoped something will now be done with it.

Pages 79–83: The FBI appears to become increasingly exasperated as months go by and the media fail to publicize DeBerry's arrest, despite repeated bureau efforts to contrive a scandal over his personal life.

TO : DIRECTOR, FBI ⟨⟩ DATE: 4/22/65

FROM : SAC, NEW YORK ⟨⟩

SUBJECT: SOCIALIST WORKERS PARTY
IS-SWP
DISRUPTION PROGRAM
(OO: NY)

ReNYlet, 3/25/64.

Referenced letter set forth a disruptive tactic
involving CLIFTON DE BERRY, who in 1964, was campaigning
as SWP candidate for President of the US. The tactic
involved release of public source material identifying
DE BERRY as having a police record, deserting one wife
and living adulterously with another, the daughter of
FARRELL DOBBS, National Secretary of the SWP.

It is felt that public knowledge of the above
would reflect adversely upon the SWP.

The Bureau approved the idea and furnished the
material to a Bureau contact. The information never was
printed, however, as far as the NYO knows.

The SWP weekly newspaper "The Militant" announced
in its 3/22/65, issue that CLIFTON DE BERRY had been nominated
as SWP candidate for mayor of NYC in the 1965 elections. He
said he intended to start his campaign early.

DE BERRY will attempt to utilize public platforms,
radio and television to spread SWP propaganda, and the
disruptive tactic proposed in relet is again regarded as
having a good potential.

The Bureau is requested to approve again the
release of the derogatory information regarding DE BERRY.

If circumstances relating to the Bureau contact preclude his using the material, the NYO will submit its recommendations regarding using this data in an anonymous mailing.

SAC, New York   5/7/65

Director, FBI

SOCIALIST WORKERS PARTY
INTERNAL SECURITY - SWP
DISRUPTION PROGRAM

Reference is made to New York letters dated 4/22/65 and
3/25/64, and Bureau letter to New York dated 9/14/64.

On two occasions the derogatory information concerning
Clifton DeBerry has been brought to the attention of Bureau
contacts. However, these contacts have not seen fit to use the
information. Therefore, no further effort will be made to obtain
a release of this information through these contacts.

New York is requested to submit a recommendation regarding
the use of this derogatory material in an anonymous letter as set
forth in referenced New York letter of 4/22/65.

NOTE:

On two occasions derogatory information concerning Clifton
DeBerry was furnished to Bureau contacts for possible use in newspapers to discredit DeBerry's campaign for the President of the
United States in 1964 on the Socialist Workers Party ticket. DeBerry
is now running for the position of mayor of New York City. New York
has suggested this derogatory material be again brought to the
attention of Bureau contacts. Inasmuch as this material was not
utilized by Bureau contacts on two previous occasions, no effort
is being made to again bring the information to the attention of
these contacts.

TO :   DIRECTOR, FBI   DATE: 10/29/65

FROM :   SAC, NEW YORK

SUBJECT: SOCIALIST WORKERS PARTY
            IS-SWP
            DISRUPTION PROGRAM

ReBulet to NY, 6/21/65.

      Relet set forth that action would be initiated at
the Seat of Government re dissemination of derogatory background
concerning CLIFTON DE BERRY, SWP Candidate for Mayor of NYC.

      DE BERRY has made several public speeches, radio
and television appearances, but the NYO has noted no questioning
of him tending to bring out his background. Similarly, there
has been no critical comment re DE BERRY in this connection in
the press.

      Since the NYC elections will be held 11/2/65, it
appears that no positive results have been obtained from
this operation.

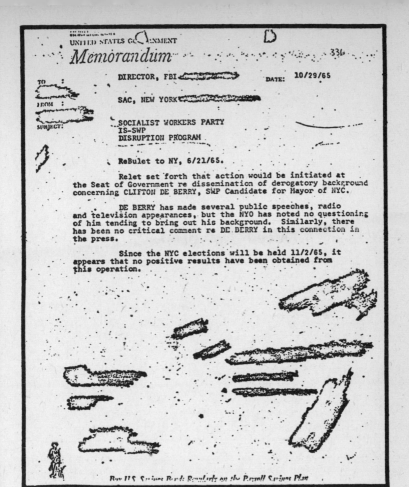

Buy U.S. Savings Bonds Regularly on the Payroll Savings Plan

4 A special hatred for Blacks

One thing that comes through clearly in the Cointelpro papers is that the FBI reserves a special hatred for the Black civil rights movement. The bureau's employment practices give a warning signal: Black special agents are only 1.2 percent of the total. And, until 1965, the only Blacks even called special agents were J. Edgar Hoover's Black personal chauffeurs, whom he dubbed "honorary special agents."

Testimony in hearings of the House Select Committee on Intelligence documented the bureau's right-wing, racist bias and showed that its political views affect its operations against activists.

Targets of the FBI's systematic sabotage of the Black movement included Dr. Martin Luther King, Jr., the Nation of Islam, Rev. Ralph Abernathy's Poor People's Campaign, Stokely Carmichael and the Black Panther party, the NAACP and the Committee to Aid the Monroe Defendants, Black members of the Socialist Workers party, and others.

One early operation began in the summer of 1961, as New York City was preparing for local elections. Since the official trade-union movement was trapped deep in the morass of Democratic party politics (where it remains today), the Socialist Workers party was offering the voters of New York an alternative. Four working-class candidates were running for the city's top positions.

The candidate for Manhattan borough president was a Black man named Clarence Franklin. "I live in a one-and-a-half-room apartment in a crowded tenement in Manhattan and I have to pay 40 percent of my total monthly wage for rent," Franklin wrote in a July issue of the *Militant*. (The socialist newsweekly editorially supports the election campaigns of the SWP.) He offered a socialist solution to New York's housing problem.

At the New York FBI office there were people who pored over that issue of the *Militant* with unusual care. J. Edgar Hoover had recently sent out special instructions for FBI agents to be alert for possible Cointelpro operations, and someone in the New York office spotted the opportunity for a vicious attack against both the Black movement and the SWP.

Clarence Franklin was born into a family of Mississippi share-croppers in 1932. When he was ten years old they moved to New York, where his mother went to work as a housecleaner. When he was fourteen he got a job setting pins in a bowling alley. Through the years Franklin found work as a dishwasher, porter, and construction laborer. Along the way he picked up an arrest record.

That fact is not very unusual; many Black workers in this society find themselves in trouble with the law—prosecuted, convicted, and imprisoned way out of proportion to their numbers in the population. One good example of this discrimination is the virtually all-Black composition of prison death rows.

There is wide recognition among socialists, civil libertarians, Black activists, and others of the racist bias of the criminal justice system. As a result, there is also growing support for the rights of the victims of this system, prisoners and former prisoners—including their right to participate in political life. But, at that time, the agents in charge of Cointelpro thought they could use Franklin's record to embarrass him and the SWP and to drive a Black activist out of politics.

One might assume that a law enforcement agency such as the FBI would have noted with satisfaction that Franklin had not been charged with violating any law in several years and was currently engaged in perfectly legal activity—running for public office.

However, the FBI had different concerns. "Careful consideration has been given to the fact that the SWP in New York City is now getting some propaganda attention through the press, television and radio because it has succeeded in placing on the ballot four candidates for office in the New York City fall elections," the FBI wrote.

In a subsequent memorandum not printed here, the FBI elaborated. "The SWP has met with little or no opposition in carrying forth its aims and purposes and in securing positions on the ballot for its candidates. It is felt that some disruptive action should be taken. . . ."

The FBI evidently used one of its numerous agents in the news media—this one at the *Daily News*—to break the "story." The *News* published a story on Franklin's arrest record on election day. It is worth noting that the rules of fair play between Democratic and Republican politicians brand as "unfair campaign practices" eleventh-hour charges that are impossible to answer before the voters go to the polling place. This, of course, did not stop the FBI.

The FBI's evaluation of this operation shows that they were elated because Franklin became demoralized by the publicity about his past. When Franklin eventually withdrew from political activity, the FBI congratulated itself on a job well done.

Sabotaging a Civil Rights Case

The next set of documents concerns a 1964 FBI plot. The aim was to sabotage the defense of a group of civil rights workers facing prison in Monroe, North Carolina.

These FBI papers accord SWP leader George Weissman the dubious distinction of being the first publicly known subject of an FBI poem. The poet tried to frame Weissman on charges of stealing money from the Monroe home of Dr. A. E. Perry, head of the Committee to Aid the Monroe Defendants (CAMD) and vice-president of the Monroe NAACP.

The poem, along with a clipping from a North Carolina newspaper showing that Weissman had been in Perry's house at the time of a robbery, was sent to a carefully selected FBI mailing list.

In 1964 George Weissman was managing editor of the *Militant*. He had first visited Monroe in 1958 to report on the notorious "kissing case." Robert F. Williams, president of the Monroe NAACP, had received attention in the press by organizing armed defense guards, which put a stop to a series of Ku Klux Klan assaults on the Black community. The Klan focused particular attention on Dr. Perry, who had been instrumental in the struggle to integrate some of Monroe's public facilities.

In retaliation against the Black community, the local racist authorities charged two Black youths, eight and ten years old, with "assault upon a white female" for the "crime" of being kissed by a white playmate.

The two were tried and committed to a reformatory "possibly until they are twenty-one."

Weissman recalled these events in a recent interview.

"I was sent down for the *Militant* and wrote several stories about the case," Weissman said. Socialists aided in the formation of the Committee to Combat Racial Injustice, and Williams became its chairman.

"The committee mounted a campaign to publicize the case of these little boys and to bring pressure on the North Carolina authorities to get them released," Weissman recalled. In a matter of months, the resulting national and international protest led to their freedom.

"In this period I became personal friends with both Williams and Perry," Weissman said, "and they often visited me when they were in New York."

Then, in August 1961, new trouble hit Monroe. This was the time of the "freedom rides," when buses filled with dedicated opponents of segregation traveled through the Deep South, challenging laws requiring separation of the races in public accommodations. Since Monroe had acquired a reputation as a Klan stronghold, it made sense for Williams to invite some of these civil rights activists to visit the city.

"A number of freedom riders on their return from Mississippi stopped off in Monroe to meet Williams and do what they could," Weissman remembered. "They decided to institute a week-long picket at the courthouse, the scene of many miscarriages of justice."

This enraged local racists, and after several days of picketing, things came to a head. On August 27 a mob attacked the picketers, and police responded by arresting the freedom riders.

"When word of this reached the Black community, the people became enraged and began preparing to defend themselves against a racist attack," Weissman said. "About this time a car carrying a middle-aged white couple from another city wandered into the Black community. Residents stopped the car and took its occupants to William's home. Williams offered to allow them to stay there until things cooled down."

The couple later left unharmed. But local authorities brought phony charges of kidnapping against Williams; Harold Reade and Richard Crowder, young Black Monroe residents; Mae Mallory, a Black woman from New York who had been working with Williams; and Robert Lowry, a white freedom rider from New York.

Williams and Mallory escaped from North Carolina, while Crowder, Reade, and Lowry were jailed in Monroe. Supporters quickly set up the CAMD to fight the anticipated extradition orders for Mallory, who was in Ohio, and Williams, whose whereabouts remained unknown, and to raise bail money for the three defendants in Monroe.

Williams soon arrived in Cuba, where he obtained asylum. The state of Ohio eventually extradited Mallory to North Carolina.

"When the case came to trial in 1964, I went down there to cover it both for the *Militant,* which gave more attention to events in Monroe than any newspaper in the country, and the *Nation* magazine," Weissman said. "I had written an article for the *Nation* at the time of the kissing case, and the editor commissioned me to do another story this time. That's how I happened to be in Monroe at the time of the robbery at Dr. Perry's home."

Perry's house served as a gathering place for supporters of the defendants during the trial.

"On this particular day, since I had to meet a *Militant* deadline, I remained in the house while others went to court," Weissman recalled.

"While I was alone in the house, there was a phone call for Dr. Perry. When I said he was not there, the caller asked me who was there besides myself. I said there was no one.

"An hour or so later the doorbell rang, and I looked out through the glass and I saw a young Black man with an envelope. I opened the door, and he said that the envelope was for Dr. Perry. When I reached to take it, he produced a pistol."

The robber directed Weissman to the basement. A second man, who Weissman did not see, entered the house. They tied Weissman to a chair and went upstairs.

"After they left, I freed myself," Weissman said. "About the same time Dr. Perry and the others returned from the trial. It turned out that a wall safe hidden in the closet had been broken into and robbed."

Since it was not unusual for doctors to keep money in their offices, this was assumed at the time to be a simple robbery. Weissman now has second thoughts about that.

"Looking back on it now, especially in view of the revelations about the methods of the FBI and the CIA, I wonder if they had a hand in it." There is no direct evidence of that in the Cointelpro documents currently available, but Weissman thinks it warrants looking into.

The documents on pages 100–104 outline this operation. In another document not reproduced here, the FBI openly stated that its goal was to "cause the SWP and CAMD to cease their efforts on behalf of the defendants."

The Monroe defendants' conviction was overturned, and the prosecution was not able to try the case again.

On January 16, 1976, fifteen years after the kidnapping indictment and one year after the Cointelpro files became public, Robert Williams was freed of all the charges against him. The North Carolina prosecutors said their witness was too ill to testify.

Williams sees it differently: "They never had a case. They didn't have a case from the beginning." He said the North Carolina authorities trumped up the charges because of his leadership in the civil rights movement.

"They knew we were planning to subpoena records and officials to expose the tactics they have been using. It would have been very embarrassing to them."

Documents from St. Louis show that the bureau also used forged, racist letters in early 1970 to split up marriages of some leaders of a civil rights group. The FBI field office sent the Black husband of a white woman working in a group called ACTION a letter, signed "A Soul Sister," alleging that his wife was having sexual relations with other men.

Five months later, the St. Louis agent in charge reported to Washington that the operation was a success. He said the FBI's efforts "certainly contributed very strongly" to the couple's separation.

Other documents, not reprinted here, reveal that in December 1970 the FBI began a program of targeting individuals it called "Key Black Extremists" (KBEs). To earn the label KBE an individual only needed to be "extremely active and most vocal" in opposition to racial discrimination, according to one document.

Another one adds: "Intensified coverage to bring to bear the total capabilities of the Bureau on investigations of these individuals is warranted. We should cover every facet of their current activities, future plans, weaknesses, strengths, and personal lives to neutralize the effectiveness of each KBE. The finances, travel, utterances, and possible violations of Federal and local law of these individuals should receive the closest investigative and supervisory attention."

In explaining the vastness of the new disruption program, J. Edgar Hoover wrote in a December 23, 1970 memo: "The term KBE does not require that an individual actually hold an official position in an organization but is to include others of equal importance because of their influence as black extremists."

During the period 1967-1971, there was an awakening of Black consciousness. Uppermost in the minds of Hoover and his associates, the documents reveal, was their desire to trammel the efforts of Black organizations to win followers.

A battery of tactics were used in this process.

• In April 1970 the bureau seized on an opportunity to disrupt relations between the Panthers and Stokely Carmichael, the group's former prime minister.

Carmichael, who resigned from the party in 1969 and was living in Africa, criticized the Panthers in a speech during a visit to the states.

The bureau wrote an account of his remarks and suggested it be "furnished to a cooperative news media source." The FBI's "news story" depicted Carmichael as having launched a "vindictive attack on the Black Panther Party organization and its black-and-white-revolution-together ideology."

The FBI wrote that Carmichael's remarks "may be used in generating additional mutual animosity between him and the Panthers to the benefit of the Bureau."

• In a February 1968 memo to Washington, the Boston FBI asked permission to supply material on the personal foibles of Nation of Islam leaders to a friendly radio talk show host. The interviewer would then twit the individuals into discussing "subjects which would be embarrassing for the NOI to answer." Hoover gave permission.

The next year, the bureau conducted a similar operation in Miami. "This exposé showed that NOI leaders are of questionable character and live in luxury through the large amount of money taken as contributions from their members," a report to Hoover said. ". . . Attendance by visitors at weekly NOI meetings has dropped 50%. This shows the value of carefully planned counterintelligence action." Hoover initialed the memo, adding, "Excellent."

• The bureau also hoped to saddle the Black Liberators of St. Louis and the Black United Front of Cairo, Illinois, with undue burdens by impugning the loyalty and morality of their leaders.

Between 1969 and 1970 the bureau circulated letters falsely

accusing activists of debauchery and of squirreling away organization funds for the purpose of high living.

Rev. Charles Koen, the leader of the Black United Front, says now that the letters "almost destroyed my marriage." He recently filed a $6 million damage suit against the bureau.

• The FBI also used a media operation against the Poor People's Campaign sponsored by the Southern Christian Leadership Conference.

The campaign, led by Rev. Ralph Abernathy, was set up to lobby Congress to end the poverty and oppression of Blacks. It eventually drew several thousand Blacks to the capital in June 1968—even though the FBI had earlier manufactured news stories to malign the effort.

"The mule train got great publicity for the poor people," one FBI story said, referring to the dramatization of the broken promise of forty acres and a mule to freed slaves, "but when it comes to the hard work of 'turning the Nation's Capital upside down,' in the words of Reverend Abernathy, the poor people invest in several thousand dollars worth of automotive equipment." (The campaign had to buy some cars to get people to Washington.)

The story added that the campaign "bought two more cars over the Memorial Day weekend, making the fleet as large as some of the car rental agencies in Washington." Another FBI "news story" on the campaign reported that in one caravan descending on the capital there were 315 unsupervised Black teenagers. Therefore, it concluded, "Washington, D.C. faces an explosive situation."

*   *   *

Blacks and others are raising serious questions about the government's version of the April 1968 slaying of Martin Luther King. Many are demanding a new investigation, especially in light of the revelation of six years of FBI schemes to discredit and destroy the famed civil rights leader.

James Earl Ray, a small-time stick-up and rackets man living in Los Angeles, got into his car one day and for no known reason drove across the country, murdered King, then fled and financed his way across two continents for three months all by himself, the government's story claims.

But as the picture of FBI harassment and surveillance of King comes out—according to a former Atlanta agent, it was so tight

King "could not wriggle his ears without the FBI knowing about it"—this version seems less and less credible.

Did the FBI's hatred of King and the Black rights struggle drive the bureau to kill him, possibly involving Ray and others? Did they provide the murder weapon or weapons, and supply Ray with perfect aliases, contacts, and the necessary funds to travel and live abroad before he was captured?

If not, the obvious question is raised: why has the bureau suppressed relevant facts about King's death?

Public doubts about the official version of King's death have deepened. Eighty percent of those polled in a recent CBS survey stated they believed Ray had help in the slaying.

Ray may or may not be telling the truth. Nevertheless, there remains a maze of questions surrounding the slaying, the answers to which might spell FBI.

To begin to find the truth, an independent investigation, led by and responsible to the Black community, is necessary.

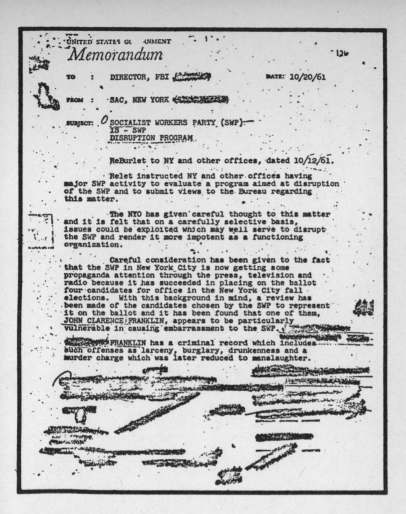

UNITED STATES GOVERNMENT

Memorandum

.126

TO : DIRECTOR, FBI

DATE: 10/20/61

FROM : SAC, NEW YORK

SUBJECT: SOCIALIST WORKERS PARTY (SWP)—
IS - SWP
DISRUPTION PROGRAM

ReBurlet to NY and other offices, dated 10/12/61.

Relet instructed NY and other offices having
major SWP activity to evaluate a program aimed at disruption
of the SWP and to submit views to the Bureau regarding
this matter.

The NYO has given careful thought to this matter
and it is felt that on a carefully selective basis,
issues could be exploited which may well serve to disrupt
the SWP and render it more impotent as a functioning
organization.

Careful consideration has been given to the fact
that the SWP in New York City is now getting some
propaganda attention through the press, television and
radio because it has succeeded in placing on the ballot
four candidates for office in the New York City fall
elections. With this background in mind, a review has
been made of the candidates chosen by the SWP to represent
it on the ballot and it has been found that one of them,
JOHN CLARENCE FRANKLIN, appears to be particularly
vulnerable in causing embarrassment to the SWP.

FRANKLIN has a criminal record which includes
such offenses as larceny, burglary, drunkenness and a
murder charge which was later reduced to manslaughter.

*Pages 93–99: An early Cointelpro operation against a
socialist candidate, which the FBI considered a model, is
outlined in these documents. The victim was a former
prisoner, a young Black worker who had come to see the
need for social change through his own experiences.
Heightened public consciousness about racism and the
nature of the courts and prisons has made such smear
tactics less effective in recent years.*

These offenses took place during the years 1949-1956 in Albany, NY, prior to the time FRANKLIN moved to NY and became connected with the SWP. As a result, his prior criminal record is not known to the rank and file of the SWP and quite possibly is also unknown to the Party leadership.

When the SWP newspaper, "The Militant", introduced FRANKLIN as a candidate, he was described as accusing the Democrats and Republicans of dipping their hands into graft and of offering himself as an alternative to this. "The Militant" further set forth that the SWP candidates were on the side of the honest and productive people of the City and against those who insisted on enjoying privileges at other people's expense.

The SWP has consistently printed that it consistently maintained a high principled position over the years and was, contrary to other radical groups, a Party of consistent integrity.

It is felt that it is quite possible a considerable disruptive effect would result if it should become public knowledge that FRANKLIN, the candidate chosen by the SWP to represent it on the ballot, was a convicted thief and murderer. It is not believed that it would be necessary to give any large display to information of this sort, there is no doubt that a short item in the back pages of a metropolitan NY newspaper would quickly become well known within the SWP and related groups. It is believed that the effect of such a public revealment could possibly result in the following:

1. Among the SWP membership, there could well be a feeling of disillusionment with the leadership of the Party for running such an individual as a candidate as well as distrust of FRANKLIN himself because of his past record.

94

2. Among the SWP's opponents in the radical field, there has always been an undercurrent of vindictive feeling and it is quite likely that the Communist Party (CP) or a rival Trotskyist group would seize upon an issue such as the FRANKLIN case to attack the principles of the SWP.

3. From the point of view from the public at large, it would seem that anyone reading an item regarding the FRANKLIN candidacy could hardly help but have a lower opinion of the SWP.

There is submitted for consideration by the Bureau a sample of the type of story which might be submitted to a friendly newspaper in this regard:

"One of the minor entries in the New York City municipal elections is the candidate of the Socialist Workers Party for Manhattan Borough President, Clarence Franklin. He was introduced in the Party's newspaper 'The Militant' in the issue of July 24 and 31, 1961, as being 'On the side of the honest productive people of the City'. Franklin accused the Democrats and Republicans of dipping their hands in graft and he offered himself as an alternative.

"In giving his background and qualifications, Franklin omitted some facts in regard to honesty and productivity which are a matter of record to the Albany Police Department. Under his full name of John Clarence Franklin, he accumulated an arrest record beginning with petit larceny in 1949, burglary and grand larceny in 1951, drunkenness in 1954 and murder in 1956.

"In especially considering its small size, it would appear the SWP takes all honors in fielding the candidate least well qualified for the office to which he aspires."

There are enclosed for the Bureau a copy of the FD 9 setting forth FRANKLIN's FBI fingerprint record and pertinent articles printed in "The Militant" of 7/24 and 31/61, regarding FRANKLIN.

It is recommended that the Bureau furnish the above information to one of its contacts in the newspaper field. However, if this course of action is not considered favorably in this instance, it is suggested that the Bureau consider allowing NY to furnish the information to a friendly newspaper in the NY area. Should this procedure be agreeable to the Bureau, a copy of the photograph of FRANKLIN taken by the Albany, NY Police Department, 7/23/52, would be furnished the newspaper contact with the suggestion that FRANKLIN be interviewed by a reporter of the newspaper in order that he may make his own determination that the individual running for public office on the SWP ticket is identical with the individual on whom the extensive criminal record exists.

For the information of the Bureau, a new file has been opened by the NYO on captioned case and this office will continue to give well thought out attention to develop all possibilities in the future which might serve to have a disruptive effect on the SWP.

SAC, New York ▓▓▓▓▓▓▓▓   October 30, 1961

Director, FBI ▓▓▓▓▓▓▓▓

SOCIALIST WORKERS PARTY
INTERNAL SECURITY - SWP
DISRUPTION PROGRAM

      Reurlet 10/20/61 captioned as above and submitting
for Bureau consideration a Disruption Program operation aimed
at causing embarrassment to the Socialist Workers Party (SWP),
its leaders and its membership.

      This suggestion is an excellent example of the type
desired by the Bureau under the Disruption Program. The Bureau
is pleased to note that the suggestion was well thought out
and it is felt that if future suggestions are submitted with
the same amount of preparation and planning, this program will
be exceedingly successful.

      The necessary action has been taken at the Bureau
to carry out your suggestion. No steps should be taken by
you concerning this operation. Should any tangible results
come to your attention as a result of Bureau-initiated action
in this matter, the Bureau should be advised promptly.

NOTE ON YELLOW:

      See cover memo ▓▓▓▓▓▓▓▓, same caption,
dated 10/27/61-, TFR:cdb.

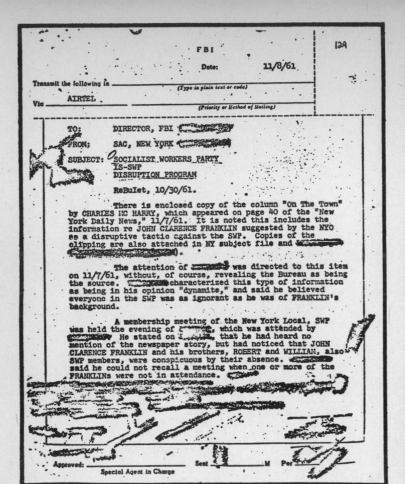

FBI

Date: 11/8/61

Transmit the following in _____

(Type in plain text or code)

Via _____ AIRTEL _____

(Priority or Method of Mailing)

TO: DIRECTOR, FBI

FROM: SAC, NEW YORK

SUBJECT: SOCIALIST WORKERS PARTY
          IS-SWP
          DISRUPTION PROGRAM

ReBulet, 10/30/61.

There is enclosed copy of the column "On The Town" by CHARLES MC HARRY, which appeared on page 40 of the "New York Daily News," 11/7/61. It is noted this includes the information re JOHN CLARENCE FRANKLIN suggested by the NYO as a disruptive tactic against the SWP. Copies of the clipping are also attached in NY subject file and

The attention of   was directed to this item on 11/7/61, without, of course, revealing the Bureau as being the source.   characterized this type of information as being in his opinion "dynamite," and said he believed everyone in the SWP was as ignorant as he was of FRANKLIN's background.

A membership meeting of the New York Local, SWP was held the evening of   , which was attended by   He stated on   , that he had heard no mention of the newspaper story, but had noticed that JOHN CLARENCE FRANKLIN and his brothers, ROBERT and WILLIAM, also SWP members, were conspicuous by their absence.   said he could not recall a meeting when one or more of the FRANKLINs were not in attendance.

Approved: _____   Sent _____ M   Per _____

Special Agent in Charge

On the Town

By CHARLES McHARRY

His Record Speaks . . .

Civic improvement expert Victor Dallaire writes: "Charlie, how are you going to vote today?" Vic, being an independent thinker, I think I'm going to jump all over the voting machine. Bob or Looie—

Anna Maria Alberghetti

I'm not sure which one at this point—will get my vote for mayor. I would love to vote for LaGuardia again, but he isn't running. The one guy I have made up my mind on is John Clarence Franklin, candidate for borough president of Manhattan on the ticket of the Socialist

Harold Minsky

Workers Party. John has accused his rivals of shameless dishonesty and general crookedness and has pictured himself as a public servant of utter probity. Here, if he cares to stand on it, is his record: Arrested for petty larceny in Albany in 1949; bagged for burglary and grand larceny in 1951; pulled in twice for drunkenness in 1954, and hit with a first degree murder rap, although the charge was reduced to manslaughter, in 1956. Seems he robbed a man and pushed him into the Hudson River, where his victim drowned. He was paroled from Clinton Prison in January, 1959. Although it would be interesting to see what Mr. Franklin would do as Manhattan's borough president, I think I'll vote for Mrs. Lawrence.

* * *

Harold Minsky, currently operating in Las Vegas, will bring burlesque back to Broadway this winter. . . . George Abbott, frowning on the Twist, told Roseland's Lou Brecker, who has banned the dance from his ballroom, that he'll never use it in any of his shows . . . Hollywood-by-the-Sea, Florida, unveils a $3-million health spa on Dec. 19. It will feature weight-reducing, rejuvenation and Roman baths, all under medical supervision. . . . Clauson

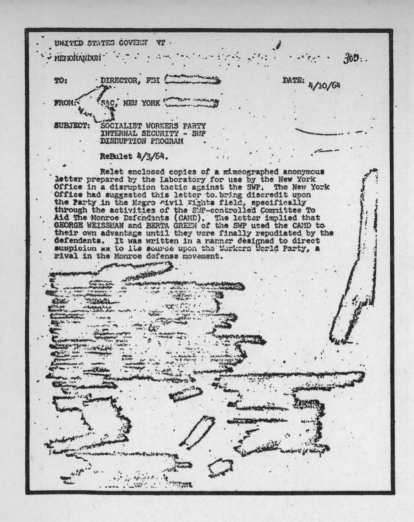

UNITED STATES GOVERNMENT
MEMORANDUM   360

TO: DIRECTOR, FBI [redacted]   DATE: 4/10/64

FROM: SAC, NEW YORK [redacted]

SUBJECT: SOCIALIST WORKERS PARTY
           INTERNAL SECURITY - SWP
           DISRUPTION PROGRAM

           ReBulet 4/3/64.

           Relet enclosed copies of a mimeographed anonymous
letter prepared by the Laboratory for use by the New York
Office in a disruption tactic against the SWP. The New York
Office had suggested this letter to bring discredit upon
the Party in the Negro civil rights field, specifically
through the activities of the SWP-controlled Committee To
Aid The Monroe Defendants (CAMD). The letter implied that
GEORGE WEISSMAN and BERTA GREEN of the SWP used the CAMD to
their own advantage until they were finally repudiated by the
defendants. It was written in a manner designed to direct
suspicion as to its source upon the Workers World Party, a
rival in the Monroe defense movement.

*Pages 100–104: An FBI scheme to sabotage defense efforts
for framed-up Monroe civil rights activists included an anonymous letter, a newspaper clipping, and a poem. These
were sent to radical publications in an effort to create the im-*

Copies of the anonymous letter were mailed on
4/8/64, in commercially purchased envelopes addressed by
a clerical employee of the New York Office. The letter
was sent to the individuals listed below:

(1) DANIEL WATTS
Editor, "Liberator"
244 East 46th Street
New York, New York

(2) HAROLD CRUSE
203 West 14th Street
New York, New York

(3) Editor, "The Worker"
23 West 26th Street
New York, New York

(4) Editor, "National Guardian"
197 East Fourth Street
New York, New York

(5) JAMES BALDWIN
470 West End Avenue
New York, New York

(6) PETER KIHSS
c/o New York Times
229 West 43rd Street
New York, New York

(7) JAMES ROBERTSON
c/o "Spartacist"
Box 1377, G.P.O.
New York, New York

(8) TIM WOHLFORTH
160 West 95th Street
New York, New York

*pression George Weissman had stolen defense committee
funds and to generate mutual suspicions within the movement. (An earlier Monroe disruption is documented on
pages 156–162.)*

(9) LEROI JONES
    27 Cooper Square
    New York, New York

     If any information re this mailing appears in
New York files designated to receive a copy of instant
letter, it should be directed to subject file, so the
Bureau can be advised.

     It is believed that a follow-up to this anonymous
mailing may increase the effectiveness of the disruption
operation. We can take advantage of the fact that GEORGE
WEISSMAN reported to the Monroe police that while he was alone
in the home of a Monroe Negro civil rights leader, two bandits
came in and rifled a wall safe. A Xerox copy of a clipping
from the Charlotte Observer of 2/27/64, outlining the
story, is enclosed for information of the Bureau.

     Since recipients of the first anonymous letter are
familiar with the connection of the SWP's WEISSMAN with the
Monroe defense, it will not be necessary to go into a
detailed exposition if they are furnished copies of the
clipping. Bureau authority is requested to send a Xerox
copy of the Charlotte Observer article to the same individuals
named above in instant letter. Bureau is also requested to
authorize enclosing with the clipping, as a device to generate
further suspicions, the following bit of verse:

          Georgie-Porgie, down in Monroe,
          Found himself alone with the dough,
          Called the cops, and what did he say?
          "Bad guys came and took it away".

     If approved, Bureau is requested to have the Laboratory
prepare the poem, as expeditiously as possible, ▰▰▰▰▰▰▰ The poem should

be on a mimeographed half-sheet, presumably an economy by the putative sender.

In addition to the addressees of the first anonymous letter, another will be added for the second letter, if approved by the Bureau. This is the editor of Progressive Labor, Box 808, G.P.O., Brooklyn 1, New York. This organization was also active in Monroe and as a rival of the SWP may be interested in the material to use in attacking the Party.

The Bureau is requested to advise the New York Office as soon as possible since interest in the Monroe case becomes less as time goes by.

Doctor's WallSafe Cracked

N.Y. Trial Reporter Only Person Home

By DON GRAY
Observer Staff Writer

MONROE — Two bandits forced their way into the home of a Monroe Negro physician Wednesday, tied up a visitor who was the only person in the house at the time, and rifled a wall safe.

The visitor was a free - lance New York City journalist, George Weissman, who was in Monroe to cover the racial kidnap trial now going on. He said the bandits, at least one of whom had a gun, ordered him to keep quiet while they robbed the safe.

The house was owned by Dr. A. E. Perry, a former president of the Monroe NAACP chapter, who said "money . . . but money" was taken from the safe. He said he did not know how much was taken.

"I'll have to do some figuring and I'll have to talk with my wife, first," he said.

Weissman said he was at the Perry house shortly before noon when he heard someone at the door. He said a Negro man was there, asking to see Perry.

Suddenly, the man pointed a pistol at him and backed him into the house. Weissman was taken to the basement, tied up, and gagged with a piece of drapery.

A second man came into the basement then, Weissman said, but he was ordered not to turn around and look.

The two men left Weissman in the basement and went to work on the safe upstairs.

Police Lt. Ted Broome said the wall safe, hidden behind clothes in a closet, was forced open with a garden pick.

Weissman said two defense lawyers and one defendant in the kidnap trial had been living at Perry's home.

He said the lawyers and some of their clients came to the house for lunch a few minutes after the robbers left.

By that time, Weissman said, he had managed to untie himself.

"There sure is a lot going on here," Weissman said. "New York City is dull compared to Monroe."

(Indicate page, name of newspaper, city and state.)

10   CHARLOTTE OBSERVER
       Charlotte, N. C.

Date: 2-27-64
Edition:
Author:
Editor:
Title:

Character
or
Classification:

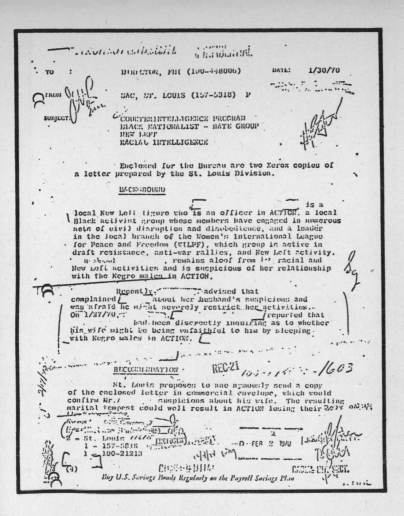

TO : DIRECTOR, FBI (100-448006)   DATE: 1/30/70

FROM : SAC, ST. LOUIS (157-5318) P

SUBJECT: COUNTERINTELLIGENCE PROGRAM
BLACK NATIONALIST - HATE GROUP
NEW LEFT
RACIAL INTELLIGENCE

Enclosed for the Bureau are two Xerox copies of
a letter prepared by the St. Louis Division.

BACKGROUND

_____ is a
local New Left figure who is an officer in ACTION, a local
Black activist group whose members have engaged in numerous
acts of civil disruption and disobedience, and a leader
in the local branch of the Women's International League
for Peace and Freedom (WILPF), which group is active in
draft resistance, anti-war rallies, and New Left activity.
_____ remains aloof from ___ racial and
New Left activities and is suspicious of her relationship
with the Negro males in ACTION.

Recently _____ advised that
complained _____ about her husband's suspicions and
was afraid he might severely restrict her activities.
On 1/27/70 _____ reported that
_____ had been discreetly inquiring as to whether
his wife might be being unfaithful to him by sleeping
with Negro males in ACTION.

RECOMMENDATION

St. Louis proposes to anonymously send a copy
of the enclosed letter in commercial envelope, which would
confirm Mr./ _____ suspicions about his wife. The resulting
marital tempest could well result in ACTION losing their _____

2 - St. Louis
1 - 157-5318
1 - 100-21213

Pages 105–107: *FBI efforts to split up a civil rights activist's
marriage included sending an anonymous salacious letter
to her husband. In a later memo reporting the couple's
separation, the St. Louis field office prepared the way for
more disruption: "Factionalism has developed within the
organization called Black Nationalism. When the best way
to capitalize on this friction is determined separate Bureau
authority will be requested for such a counterintelligence
operation."*

SL 157-5818

Corresponding Secretary and the WILPF losing a
valuable leader, thus striking a major blow against
both organizations.

Bureau authority is requested to initiate
this activity.

Dear M.,

Look man I guess your old lady dosen't get enough at home or she wouldn't be shucking and jiving with our Black Men in ACTION, you dig? Like all she wants to intergrate is the bed room ~~and the~~ Black Sisters ain't gonna take no second best from our men. So lay it on her, man — or get her the hell off Newstead.

A Soul Sister

FROM   Walter Yeagley, Assistant Attorney General
        Internal Security Division

SUBJECT: NATION OF ISLAM
         INTERNAL SECURITY - NOI

CONFIDENTIAL

This is in reply to your memorandum to the Attorney General
dated September 9, 1960, inquiring about the possibility of pro-
secutive action against the leaders or designation of the captioned
organization under provisions of Executive Order No. 10450.

The available evidence concerning the activities of the
leaders and members of this organization falls far short of the
evidentiary requirements sufficient to meet the standards set forth
in the Yates decision. While the leaders of the NOI at times re-
sort to the use of virulent and vicious language which would incite
the members to individual acts of violence against the white race,
it is more calculated and designed to arouse hatred and antipathy
against the white race as a race, rather than against the Government.
There is evidence of language which speaks of the destruction of
America, but is couched more in terms of prophecy and prediction,
often referring to the "War of Armageddon," than in terms of incite-
ment to action. Moreover, the First Amendment would require
something more than language of prophecy and prediction and implied
threats against the Government to establish the existence of a
clear and present danger to the nation and its citizens.

Regarding designation of the NOI pursuant to the provision
of Executive Order 10450, it is our opinion that hate-language employed by the organization's leaders is not probative of the criteria
of "subversive" nor is it sufficient to establish the NOI to be an
organization ". . . seeking to alter the form of government by
unconstitutional means." Although there is substantial evidence of
NOI's advocacy of future violent reprisals for alleged wrongs committed against one or more of its members, the evidence is
insufficient at this time to meet the criterion that it has adopted
a policy of advocating or approving the commission of such acts
of violence to deny others their constitutional rights.

5 SEP 26 1960

CONFIDENTIAL

---

*Pages 108–109: A memo from the Justice Department dated
September 23, 1960, telling J. Edgar Hoover that the Nation
of Islam is a legal organization and can't be prosecuted for
anything. The Justice Department, in spite of its findings,
did ask the bureau to "continue its investigation of the*

Just stalling!

H

group." Hoover was unsatisfied with the Justice Department's instructions, scribbled "Just stalling!" on the memo, and went ahead with Cointelpro operations against the legal organization.

5 "Drive a wedge between the followers of Malcolm X and the SWP"

The murder of Dr. Martin Luther King, Jr., is not the only murder of a Black leader that remains unsolved.

There are many more questions than answers about the assassination in February 1965 of Malcolm X—questions, for example, about the possible role of the New York City police, the FBI, and the CIA. To many in 1965, these questions seemed farfetched. But suspicions that might have seemed outlandish then—before the American people learned about Cointelpro and the CIA's domestic operations—today not only seem reasonable but also demand answers.

Yet the multitude of inquiries by Congressional committees and other government-sponsored investigations into FBI and CIA crimes haven't even touched on the case of Malcolm X.

None of the FBI's files about its activities against Malcolm X have yet been made public. Some Cointelpro memos reprinted here show the FBI's attempt to poison relations after Malcolm's death between the groups he founded and the Socialist Workers party. These memos hint at some FBI interference in Malcolm's organizations before his death.

It is worth looking at the views and activities of Malcolm X, especially during his last year, to get an idea of why the FBI was interested in him and why it wanted to disrupt the relationship between his followers and the SWP.

All during his last year, Malcolm's views became more and more militant. After several months of silence imposed on him for making statements that Black Muslim leader Elijah Muhammad frowned on, Malcolm X broke discipline with remarks the whole world heard.

The gun, it was said, made an awesome sound.

The government had not finished their work with Malcolm's death. They continued to pursue his followers, as the files reprinted here show. The bureau saw an opportunity both to give Black militants a false picture of the SWP's relationship with Malcolm and to prevent unified actions by Blacks and socialists.

In a May 25, 1965, letter to the New York office, Hoover wrote: "It would appear that the apparent attempt by the SWP to exploit the followers of the late Malcolm X for its own benefit offers some potential for the institution of disruptive tactics."

On June 15, 1965, New York responded: "SWP influence on the followers of MALCOLM X would be disrupted by emphasizing the atheism of the SWP as opposed to the basic religious orientation of the MMI." (Malcolm created the Muslim Mosque, Inc., MMI, and the Organization of Afro-American Unity, OAAU, after his break with the Nation of Islam. The Mosque was for Muslim activists, but the OAAU did not require religious adherence for membership.)

Washington approved the recommendation.

In August 1965 the New York office wrote to Hoover boasting that the operation had sabotaged cooperation between the socialists and Malcolm's followers.

"It is believed probable that the disintegrating relations between the SWP and [the OAAU] can be attributed to the disruptive tactic authorized . . . and will result in a continued loss of influence by the SWP among this group of Negroes."

Harlem activist Charles Kenyatta, who was prominent among Malcolm's followers, has called the Cointelpro tactics "criminal," but is not surprised at these revelations.

"When you have one man who was as great as Malcolm was, then you can expect these FBI and CIA tactics against him and his followers."

The exact circumstances of Malcolm X's death, however, remain a mystery. Some have suggested setting up an independent commission of inquiry, responsible to the Black community.

There have been such commissions before. And they have produced some important results.

A Black commission was set up in Detroit in the early part of 1973 to look into police terror against Blacks by the self-styled "anticrime" unit known as STRESS. The commission's findings and community protests soon prompted police officials to dismantle STRESS.

Another Black commission was created after the police slaughter of Black students at Southern University in Louisiana in 1972. That fourteen-member body found solid evidence of police guilt; and even the governor of Louisiana felt compelled to testify before it.

An independent commission to investigate the murder of Malcolm X could demand access to the still-secret files on the assassination. It could help answer why certain statements by Malcolm's convicted killer were not pursued at the trial—statements that he was hired by an unnamed person, not a Muslim, to murder Malcolm. (The police tried at the time to make it seem that the Muslims murdered Malcolm in an internecine struggle.) It could possibly answer questions. Why were the police films of the events at the scene when Malcolm was murdered never shown during the trial? What were "several" members of a secret "subversives" unit of the New York police department doing among the audience when Malcolm was killed? (The head of the squad admitted some of its agents were there.)

The answers to these and other questions are there, in the secret files of the FBI, yet to be exposed.

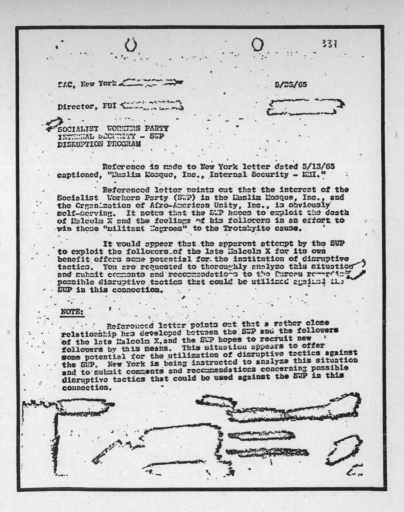

SAC, New York _____ 5/25/65

Director, FBI _____

SOCIALIST WORKERS PARTY
INTERNAL SECURITY - SWP
DISRUPTION PROGRAM

Reference is made to New York letter dated 5/13/65 captioned, "Muslim Mosque, Inc., Internal Security - MMI."

Referenced letter points out that the interest of the Socialist Workers Party (SWP) in the Muslim Mosque, Inc., and the Organization of Afro-American Unity, Inc., is obviously self-serving. It notes that the SWP hopes to exploit the death of Malcolm X and the feelings of his followers in an effort to win these "militant Negroes" to the Trotskyite cause.

It would appear that the apparent attempt by the SWP to exploit the followers of the late Malcolm X for its own benefit offers some potential for the institution of disruptive tactics. You are requested to thoroughly analyze this situation and submit comments and recommendations to the Bureau regarding possible disruptive tactics that could be utilized against the SWP in this connection.

NOTE:

Referenced letter points out that a rather close relationship has developed between the SWP and the followers of the late Malcolm X, and the SWP hopes to recruit new followers by this means. This situation appears to offer some potential for the utilization of disruptive tactics against the SWP. New York is being instructed to analyze this situation and to submit comments and recommendations concerning possible disruptive tactics that could be used against the SWP in this connection.

Pages 115–118: The FBI has not released any documents on its operations against Malcolm X and his followers in the period leading up to his assassination, but this bureau correspondence dated just after his death indicates an intense interest in the Muslim Mosque, Inc., founded by Malcolm. The operation outlined here is occasioned by New York's alarm that "a rather close relationship has developed between the SWP and the followers of the late Malcolm X." The next communication notes with satisfaction that the groups he led "have been declining in strength and influence" since his death and proposes to use undercover agents within the Black movement to sow discord.

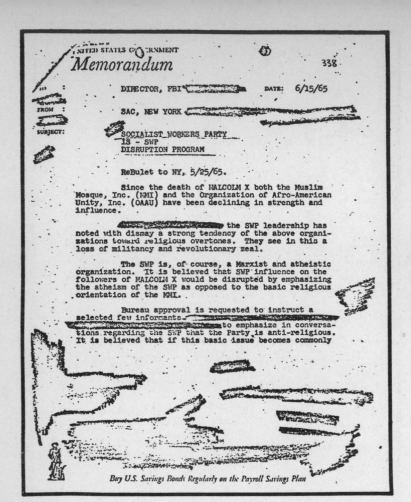

UNITED STATES GOVERNMENT

Memorandum

338

TO : DIRECTOR, FBI ▮▮▮▮▮▮▮▮▮ DATE: 6/15/65

FROM : SAC, NEW YORK ▮▮▮▮▮▮▮▮▮▮▮

SUBJECT: SOCIALIST WORKERS PARTY
IS - SWP
DISRUPTION PROGRAM

ReBulet to NY, 5/25/65.

Since the death of MALCOLM X both the Muslim Mosque, Inc. (MMI) and the Organization of Afro-American Unity, Inc. (OAAU) have been declining in strength and influence.

▮▮▮▮▮▮▮▮▮▮▮▮ the SWP leadership has noted with dismay a strong tendency of the above organizations toward religious overtones. They see in this a loss of militancy and revolutionary zeal.

The SWP is, of course, a Marxist and atheistic organization. It is believed that SWP influence on the followers of MALCOLM X would be disrupted by emphasizing the atheism of the SWP as opposed to the basic religious orientation of the MMI.

Bureau approval is requested to instruct a selected few informants ▮▮▮▮▮▮▮▮▮▮▮▮ to emphasize in conversations regarding the SWP that the Party is anti-religious. It is believed that if this basic issue becomes commonly

Buy U.S. Savings Bonds Regularly on the Payroll Savings Plan

116

6

known as a point of difference, it would serve to drive
a wedge between the followers of MALCOLM X and the SWP,
thus foiling efforts of the Party to recruit in this
Negro field.

117

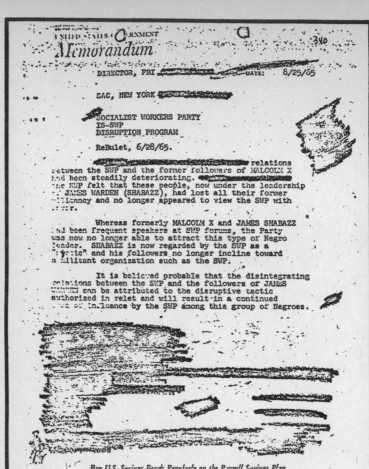

UNITED STATES GOVERNMENT

Memorandum

DIRECTOR, FBI ~~~~~~~~~~~~~~~~~~~~~~~~~ DATE: 8/25/65

SAC, NEW YORK ~~~~~~~~~~~~~~~~~~~~~~

SOCIALIST WORKERS PARTY
IS-SWP
DISRUPTION PROGRAM

ReBulet, 6/28/65.

~~~~~~~~~~~~~~~~~~~~~~~~~~~~~~~~~ relations
between the SWP and the former followers of MALCOLM X
had been steadily deteriorating. ~~~~~~~~~~~~~~~~~
the SWP felt that these people, now under the leadership
of JAMES WARDEN (SHABAZZ), had lost all their former
militancy and no longer appeared to view the SWP with
favor.

　　　　Whereas formerly MALCOLM X and JAMES SHABAZZ
had been frequent speakers at SWP forums, the Party
was now no longer able to attract this type of Negro
leader. SHABAZZ is now regarded by the SWP as a
"mystic" and his followers no longer incline toward
a militant organization such as the SWP.

　　　　It is believed probable that the disintegrating
relations between the SWP and the followers of JAMES
~~~~~~~ can be attributed to the disruptive tactic
authorized in relet and will result in a continued
~~~ of influence by the SWP among this group of Negroes.

Buy U.S. Savings Bonds Regularly on the Payroll Savings Plan

118

6 "Cause disruption in the peace movement"

For over a decade, the most explosive issue in world politics was the American war against Vietnam. It was the growing mass opposition to the war among the American people that gave the radicalization of the sixties and seventies its biggest push.

With the American withdrawal and the fall of the Saigon dictatorship in the spring of 1975, people in all parts of the political spectrum began assessing the Vietnam War era. The revelation of the FBI's schemes against the antiwar movement provides an interesting sidelight to that review. It also helps confirm the analysis the SWP made at the beginning of the movement—that it could pose a serious threat to the power of the Pentagon and Wall Street and eventually force the government to pull out of Vietnam.

The Cointelpro papers reveal several instances of behind-the-scenes FBI maneuvers to block the development of a massive visible protest movement against the war. A variety of techniques were employed to achieve this task.

These included promoting splits among antiwar forces, encouraging red-baiting of socialists, and pushing violent confrontations as an alternative to massive, peaceful demonstrations.

One of the more unusual operations uncovered to date is a 1966 FBI attempt to divert the Socialist Workers party from its strong commitment to the antiwar struggle.

The FBI mailed out an anonymous "Open Letter to Trotskyites." That and related documents are reproduced here. The letter was designed to create dissatisfaction within the party over its participation in the new movement. In particular, the FBI sought to create dissension within the SWP and Young Socialist

Alliance over their role at a November 1965 antiwar conference in Washington, D.C.

The mass movement against the war in Vietnam, and socialist participation in it, had begun with a call by the Students for a Democratic Society for an April 1965 March on Washington. SDS in 1965 possessed a measure of respectability. Officially, it was still the youth group of the League for Industrial Democracy, a longtime meeting ground for conservative social democrats and union bureaucrats. Consequently, the SDS National Council's decision to call the march, made at its meeting over the December 1964 school break, carried some authority.

Doug Jenness joined the staff of the YSA national office that January. "We met with Clark Kissinger, the SDS national secretary, to discuss what we could do," he recalls. "The YSA organized three national tours—one on the West Coast, one in the Midwest, and I toured the Eastern states." YSA locals across the country quickly began to help organize student participation in the march.

During that winter, Lyndon Johnson escalated the war, and the impact helped to turn out 20,000 people, more than anyone had expected.

"The day after the march I attended an SDS National Council meeting there in Washington," Jenness said. "Surprisingly, they failed to follow up on their original initiative." SDS pulled away from the antiwar movement and never again focused its energies on a national level toward the war.

Nevertheless, the antiwar movement continued to grow. The teach-in movement, born on March 24 at the University of Michigan, spread spontaneously from campus to campus.

In late May, the Berkeley, California, Vietnam Day Committee, in which the SWP and YSA played a role, brought out 30,000 people for a thirty-four-hour marathon teach-in and protest against the war.

Meeting in Washington, D.C., August 6–9, a national antiwar gathering, the Assembly of Unrepresented People, as it was called, drew some 2,000 participants. There a much smaller meeting of antiwar activists from around the country decided to set up a National Coordinating Committee to End the War in Vietnam. The NCC scheduled a convention during the Thanksgiving weekend in Washington, D.C. This is the conference referred to in the FBI's "Open Letter."

The socialist assessment of the antiwar movement is contained in *Revolutionary Strategy in the Fight Against the Vietnam War,* a collection of articles and documents recently published by the SWP National Education Department.

It contains a transcript of a June 25, 1965, SWP Political Committee discussion that envisioned the main lines along which the movement would develop.

Jack Barnes, who is today the SWP national secretary, described the main divisions that would emerge within the movement. "They'll be over the question of exclusion versus non-exclusion and the question of unconditional opposition to the war. They'll take place over the question of subordinating the demands of the antiwar movement to the demands of 'progressive' politicians."

Drawing their initial inspiration from preparations for the April 17 march and then spurred on by the continuing escalation of both the war and antiwar activity, there was a proliferation of "Committees to End the War in Vietnam," or "CEWV's." They looked to the upcoming Thanksgiving conference as the first real opportunity to meet on a national level, compare notes, and chart future activity.

The gathering was marked by a major dispute, one that was confusing to most of the people there. The form of the fight was over a seemingly simple organizational matter, but in the background loomed two entirely different perspectives for the future of the new movement. In reality, a fundamental question was involved—whether the antiwar movement would remain and grow as an independent force in American political life or whether it would be channeled into Democratic party politics, a graveyard for social protest movements.

From the new independent antiwar committees had come a number of people, including many SWP and YSA members, who were interested in discussing the possibility of forming a national organization composed of committees standing for immediate withdrawal of American troops from Vietnam. The NCC did not purport to be such an organization—its purpose being to coordinate activities of all sorts of organizations opposed to the war, most of which at that time favored calling for a negotiated settlement.

The SWP and YSA did not propose eliminating the role of the NCC. They recognized a place for an organization that drew all opponents of the war together for common action, but they also saw a place in the coalition for a formation of independent committees favoring immediate withdrawal.

A proposal to add a workshop to the conference agenda for

participants interested in setting up such an organization was met by an almost hysterical response from the conference steering committee. To the thousands who have over the years attended subsequent national antiwar conferences, where the right to hold the workshop of one's choice was accepted as a matter of course, this may seem hard to believe.

But the steering committee, in which the Communist party had a major influence, steadfastly refused to allow a "thirteenth" workshop. Those upholding what they saw to be their democratic right to meet on a question of mutual interest were forced to hold a "caucus" to discuss the subject.

Charges of "Trotskyite splitters and wreckers" were hurled left and right in order to obscure any rational discourse on the matter in dispute. The "splitter and wrecker" chorus continued for some time in several periodicals and in radical circles around the country.

Among the most vocal was the Communist party. Their perspective for the new movement was to send it out to ring doorbells for various Democratic "peace candidates." The Stalinists correctly saw a national organization of independent committees calling for immediate withdrawal as an obstacle to that goal. The CP's insistence on the negotiation slogan, which the SWP said violated the right of the Vietnamese to settle their own affairs, was tied in with their Democratic party orientation, since it was a demand that many liberal Democratic candidates found acceptable.

The political questions in dispute would be widely discussed in the coming months and years. Over time the antiwar movement would come to support immediate withdrawal, the demand most in line with the needs of both the American and Vietnamese peoples.

Supporters of an organization of independent committees favoring withdrawal were among the founders of the Student Mobilization Committee to End the War in Vietnam in 1966.

The political fight at the Thanksgiving weekend conference in Washington had an important positive result for the antiwar movement, in spite of the FBI's interference. Without the eventual clarity over the course of the movement that emerged from the conference, it is safe to say that this country would not have seen the massive movement that, combined with the heroic struggle of the Vietnamese, forced the United States out.

The FBI, of course, was unable to get the SWP and YSA to

pull out of the movement. Ignoring the "advice" of the FBI, the socialists discussed and drew their own conclusions.

Among the most useful for understanding the conference as a turning point in the antiwar movement was the contribution made by SWP founder James P. Cannon before the Los Angeles chapter of the SWP in December 1965. His remarks also help explain the role of the SWP in helping to build the antiwar movement.

The NCC conference marked the first head-on confrontation between the new generation of SWP members and the Communist party. Cannon thought this was significant. Referring to the "Bring the Troops Home Now" slogan, he said, "I think our comrades were correct to adopt that slogan and their militancy at the conference and their refusal to be bluffed or bulldozed is quite admirable. All the more so that they were perhaps taken by surprise and hadn't had previous experience with what the perfidy of Stalinism and the Social Democracy is really like. I will guarantee you that they will never be taken by surprise again.

"These are permanent assets which speak well for the future."

His observation seems even more true now. "Out of [the antiwar movement] I think we can see the beginnings of a new radical movement which raises great perspectives of world-historical significance for America."

*　　　*　　　*

It was not inevitable that a mass movement against the war in Vietnam would develop in this country. In fact, the life of the organized antiwar movement was characterized by frequent reevaluations of perspectives. On more than one occasion questions of strategy were posed that had life-and-death implications for the movement.

Their opponents within the antiwar movement would sometimes accuse members of the Socialist Workers party and the Young Socialist Alliance of possessing limited imagination. This charge stemmed from the Socialists' continuing insistence on mass demonstrations as the way to end the war.

In the end, however, it turned out not to be the socialists who were short on imagination, but those who lacked confidence in the possibility of the American people taking to the streets in large numbers to demand an end to the war.

It is now clear that the rulers of this country watched the development of the antiwar movement very closely. We have direct evidence that on at least several occasions the FBI sought to intervene in the political life of the movement in order to widen splits and to further trends that were harmful to its growth.

Not satisfied with Cointelpro operations against individual students and professors, or against campus organizations, the FBI targeted an entire college—actually, an entire town—for a disruption plot. Student activists at Antioch College in Yellow Springs, Ohio, had aroused the ire of the FBI watchdogs in Cincinnati. In a June 1968 memo they labeled Antioch a "center for New Left activity."

The Cincinnati office explained that such groups as the Socialist Workers party, the Young Socialist Alliance, Students for a Democratic Society, and "Black Power" had adherents on the campus. (There was no charge that any of these groups had engaged in any illegal activity.) "In . . . protest-type demonstrations of a national character," the memo noted, "Antioch and Yellow Springs have been represented by numbers exceeding their enrollment and population."

The Cincinnati office recommended that the FBI check on the "achievement" of thirty to forty radicals who had left the school. If their level of achievement was "low," this information would be fed to a friendly reporter on a Cincinnati paper.

The FBI wanted to put the Antioch administration on the spot and force it to "curtail the activities of those students . . . engaging in antisocial activity, protest demonstrations, and affiliation with subversive groups."

Of particular interest to many in the movements for social change is a memo dated July 1968, addressed to all FBI offices and signed by FBI Director Hoover: "Since the use of marijuana . . . is widespread among members of the New Left, you should be alert to opportunities to have them arrested by local authorities on drug charges. Any information concerning the fact that individuals have marijuana . . . should be immediately furnished to local authorities and they should be encouraged to take action." The FBI also encouraged cracking down on antiwar GI coffeehouses by passing along information about drug use to local cops. The government has shown it will use all the means at its disposal to silence political opposition, and locking up radicals on drug charges is one way they do it.

The FBI portrayed the Black struggle and the student antiwar movement as terrorist conspiracies in order to justify stepping up its repressive measures. In September 1970, an FBI memo declared: "Terrorist violence is all around us and more has been threatened. . . . Bombings, assassination of police officers, kidnapping and torture murder are all part of the picture. These violence-oriented black and white savages are at war with the Government and the American people."

Hoover decided to escalate this "war" by setting up a vast network of campus informers. He ordered FBI offices around the country to "immediately institute an aggressive policy of developing new productive informants who can infiltrate the ranks of terrorist organizations, their collectives, communes and staffs of their underground newspapers."

It is clear now that these campus spies infiltrated groups that had nothing whatever to do with terrorism, such as organizations that opposed the war in Vietnam, Black student groups, and socialist organizations. In fact, we now know that where there was terrorism and violence—either against government institutions or against radicals—the odds are that the FBI was involved in it.

The FBI also had another approach to harassing campus activists. The plan was to encourage conservative state legislators to crack down on the state campuses.

In 1969, for example, Hoover approved a plan devised by the Newark office for an anonymous mailing to a New Jersey state senator. The mailing would contain a copy of *Screw* magazine, available on campus, and a phony letter signed "A Concerned Student," asking the senator to do something about the distribution of "filth."

In addition, the FBI letter called to the senator's attention a short story in *Evergreen Review* that some professors of literature had distributed to their classes at Paterson State College. An FBI memo informed Hoover that the story contained "79 obscene terms referring to incest, sexuality and biology, four dozen 'cuss' words and a dozen instances of taking the Lord's name in vain."

The Newark office believed the operation would give the bureau "an opportunity . . . to focus lawmakers' attention on the depraved nature of the type of student now infesting campus activities as exemplified by New Left adherents."

Just what connection *Screw*, not to mention the short story, had to do with the "New Left" was not explained.

A similar episode occurred in 1968 when the San Antonio office devised a plan to send a newspaper clipping on communal living at the University of Texas to several state officials, along with an anonymous cover letter.

A fake student newsletter, which the FBI called *Armageddon News,* also figured in the bureau's two-year-long campaign to destroy the antiwar movement, the YSA, and other radical groups at Indiana University in Bloomington.

Published surreptitiously over two semesters, the newsletter's purpose, according to the FBI, was to "prevent any nonLeftist students from being duped into joining the groups of the New Left."

In a memo not reproduced in this book, FBI headquarters told the Indianapolis field office that "the next issue (Volume 1, Number 2) and subsequent material must contain a more sophisticated approach with regards to the situation at Indiana University and in relation to the broad protest movement in this country. Your leaflet should be prepared ostensibly by students who, while disagreeing with the Vietnam war policy and so forth, nevertheless deplore subversive elements on and off campus who are using these issues for their own purposes."

Despite such efforts by Washington to edit it into an apparently liberal-leaning publication with some appeal to the students it was aimed at, *Armageddon News* came off as a right-wing scandal sheet, as the reproduction included in this chapter shows. According to former students at Indiana University, it had zero impact on the antiwar movement there.

In addition to publishing and distributing the newsletter, the FBI infiltrated the YSA in Bloomington in order to bring about a "split in philosophy" in what it characterized as the only group on campus with a "degree of organizational structure."

In another case, in Atlanta, the FBI intervened in order to reopen a split that was in the process of being healed. The FBI feared that, after a period of disagreement in the local antiwar coalition, the Revolutionary Youth Movement (RYM, a split-off from the Students for a Democratic Society) was going to cooperate with the YSA in organizing antiwar activities. To try to prevent this, the Atlanta FBI sent an anonymous letter to a RYM leader charging manipulation of RYM by the "Trots."

During August 1968, the FBI mailed out an anonymous leaflet purporting to be from a supporter of the Radical Organizing Committee. The ROC was a short-lived organization formed by Communist party members and others who, after unsuccessfully attempting to exclude members of the YSA from the national staff of the Student Mobilization Committee to End the War in Vietnam, themselves left the SMC.

The leaflet praises those who split from the SMC and red-baits the YSA for "committee packing and other high handed crap so neatly done by the Trotskyites."

At the center of this controversy were Kipp Dawson and Syd Stapleton, two YSA members on the SMC staff who had become prominent antiwar leaders. Dawson now works as a printer, and Stapleton is national secretary of the Political Rights Defense Fund, which is sponsoring the suit that pried loose the evidence of FBI intrigue. In an interview, they talked about the 1968 dispute in light of the news about the FBI's role.

The SMC had been established in the fall of 1966 by a variety of forces, among them members of the Young Socialist Alliance, radical pacifists, and members of the Communist party and of its youth group at the time—the DuBois Clubs. The CP had from the beginning been a reluctant partner in the coalition, in part because its participation violated its traditional sectarian taboo against working with "Trotskyites."

By 1968 the SMC had already established itself as a major organization, with chapters on many campuses. It had brought out thousands of young people on the day of the largest demonstration held up to that time—April 15, 1967.

"Where the CP was headed didn't come out in a clear way until the 1967 year-end SMC convention in Chicago," Stapleton remembered. "They put forward a number of proposals that would have shifted the emphasis of the SMC away from the war. The effect would have been to turn it into a liberal youth group that dealt with many issues. During the approaching election campaign, such a group could easily swing into supporting liberal Democrats."

Things didn't come to a head until after the successful SMC-sponsored student strike against the war in April 1968. The election pressure was building, and the Eugene McCarthy presidential campaign was beginning to attract some antiwar activists. At the same time, the United States opened peace talks with the Vietnamese in Paris as part of a move to defuse antiwar sentiment. Some opponents of the war thought negotiations would bring a rapid end to the fighting.

"A controversy broke out in the 'working committee,' which was a semiofficial body of SMC members living in New York," Dawson recalled. "It was decided that no member of any political 'tendency' or group would be allowed on the SMC staff. That meant Syd and I were fired."

The antiwar movement had been based on "nonexclusion," the idea that all opponents of the war were welcome regardless of their political affiliation. The Stalinists of the Communist party defended this new step, which reversed that policy, in a variety of ways, often contradictory or illogical. For example, Mike Zagarell said YSAers should be excluded because their work had succeeded in "narrowing" the coalition.

What was really happening, of course, was that the CP was trying to transform the SMC into a support group for liberal Democratic "peace candidates," as they were called. They needed to get rid of the YSA to make that possible.

"The working committee resolution was adopted with the backing of pacifists, the Communist party, and their supporters," Stapleton said. "They had a mechanical majority."

This action brought a wave of protests from SMC members around the country. The CP and the rest of the exclusionists had opened the fight on a narrow organizational level, with the political differences submerged. They continued this by refusing to schedule an SMC convention in the Midwest, which had been mandated by the previous SMC convention. Finally, an SMC Continuations Committee meeting was set in New York—the main base of the exclusionists.

"They had tried in every way imaginable to avoid an open political discussion of the issues," Dawson said. "Now 400 people were gathered at the continuations committee meeting. The discussion was at last beginning. Suddenly, a thirty-three-year-old public relations man named Art Goldberg, who had somehow gotten himself on the SMC working committee, jumped up on a table and shouted, 'This is a Trotskyite-dominated conference! All the independents are leaving!' "

A minority began walking out, chanting, "Up against the wall!" They were met by a counter-chant of "Bring the troops home now!"

"The whole fight was summed up by the chants that came from the two sides," Stapleton remarked. "The FBI's leaflet was definitely in their style."

The SMC went on to become bigger than ever. In the fall of 1969, and then in the spring of 1971, it was the co-organizer of the biggest antiwar demonstrations in American history. Its February 1970 conference drew almost 4,000.

What happened to those who walked out? Sixty of them met at a New York church to discuss what to do. As one of them aptly put it, "Although we all feel like brothers because we all hate the Trots, that isn't enough of a basis for a new organization." Phyllis Kalb of the CP summed up the mood there. "I'm against

the YSA concept of mass demonstrations. I'm just tired of them."
They finally decided to form the Radical Organizing Committee.

"The last I heard of ROC was during the demonstrations at the Democratic party convention in Chicago that summer," Stapleton said. "I spotted two people passing out a ROC leaflet."

Stapleton recalled a later incident. "I was in Washington in the beginning of 1975, at a picket line demanding an end to continued funding for the fighting in Vietnam. A person I didn't know walked up to me and said, 'I just wanted to let you know that you were right.' 'Right about what?' I asked. 'You were right about the war in 1968,' he replied. 'You see, those of us who set up ROC really thought the war was over. I thought it had ended and it was time to go on to other issues. But it turned out you were correct.' "

Immediately prior to the April 5, 1969, antiwar demonstrations, the FBI mailed out another leaflet to an unknown number of individuals and groups that were opposed to the war. "Notes from the Sand Castle," as it was titled, red-baited the YSA and SWP and criticized them for failing to take on the "pigs."

Would such a leaflet have had any credibility? Unfortunately, it probably would because in it the FBI advocated a viewpoint that enjoyed some support at the time, primarily in circles around Students for a Democratic Society. The anonymous author claimed to be an SDS member.

In the leaflet the FBI argued in favor of violent confrontations. The following June SDS would break up, and the strongest advocates of these tactics would become the Weathermen.

When the SDS National Council opened its March 28-30 meeting in Austin, Texas, that year, the 200 delegates and several hundred more observers were handed an open letter from the YSA. "The central task of revolutionary youth right now," the YSA wrote, "is to build the April 5-6 demonstrations [against the war] as large and as militant as possible." By "militant" demonstrations, the YSA meant the kind that could involve the largest number of people opposed to the war. And those were the marches that were legal, peaceful, independent of partisan politics, nonconfrontational, and in which participants could carry their own signs and slogans for ending the war.

Building those kinds of demonstrations was precisely what YSA members around the country were doing. But the SDS gathering had what they considered to be more important business before them.

The Austin meeting marked a turning point for SDS. For several years, the Progressive Labor party, then the country's largest Maoist group, had been an increasingly important factor in the political life of SDS. With the deepening radicalization on campus, the grouping around the SDS national office was having more and more trouble responding to the political questions raised by the PLP.

At Austin they were ready to unveil the weapon they hoped would meet the PLP's challenge. They unexpectedly emerged as full-fledged followers of Chairman Mao himself, and of Stalin too. It was really just about that simple. Why let the PLP have a monopoly on Mao Tse-tung thought?

It was here that Robert Avakian, now leader of the Revolutionary Communist party, made his national debut as an exponent of Maoism. The same is true of SDS national office member Mike Klonsky, today an officer of the October League.

The Maoists have tried to portray themselves as the most ardent defenders of the Vietnamese revolution. It is worth noting that in Austin not only did they fail to endorse the April action, SDS did nothing at all about the war.

Nevertheless, the demonstrations turned out to be quite significant and sizable. New York saw 100,000 march in the rain. There were 50,000 in San Francisco, 30,000 in Chicago, 4,000 in Atlanta, and more in other cities.

They served notice on the ruling class that the American people were not taken in by the negotiations in Paris. Nixon's talk of an impending "settlement" was not going to get him off the hook.

It is no exaggeration to say that it was the stubborn persistence of the SWP and YSA and others who agreed with them in arguing for the tactic of mass peaceful protests that kept the movement alive. Ultimately, the FBI and those that it serves were unable to hold the movement back from its goal.

ReNYlet to Director, 1/17/66.

On 11/25-28/65, the National Committee to End the War in Viet Nam held a convention in Washington, D.C. The SWP and the YSA's efforts to dominate and control this convention by forcing the issue of "Immediate Withdrawal of US Troops from Viet Nam" as the basic slogan for anti-war work was soundly defeated at this conference. In addition, the YSA received considerable unfavorable publicity for its tactics and attitude at this convention.

It is felt that the above defeat by the party and youth can be of significant nature in regard to captioned program. This is pointed out by the fact that DICK FRASER, a National Committee member of the SWP from Seattle, recently directed a denunciation of the policies of the party and its youth in regard to anti-war work in writing and also at the recently-concluded SWP National Committee Plenum held during February, 1966.

Pages 131–136: As the movement against the Vietnam War developed, the Socialist Workers party and the Young Socialist Alliance came to play a leading role in its left wing, eventually winning the majority of the movement over to their concept of holding massive, peaceful demonstrations for immediate withdrawal of U.S. forces. This operation's central aim was to demoralize members over a supposed series of failures in order to "seriously hamper" their efforts to build the antiwar movement.

.2.   In all probability, the recent split of the Seattle
Branch from the party together with the possible future splits
of other branches and/or individual members is based in
part on disagreements with the party leadership on antiwar policy.

Viewed in the light of the party's unsuccessful
endeavors in various fields during the past decade, this
recent venture appears to culminate a series of leadership
policies which have caused dissention and rifts within the
party.

To exploit this, an anonymous letter has been prepared
which could be directed nationally to selected party
members who have some misgivings in regard to the leadership and direction of the party; however, to date,
have not definitely made a break.

This letter would subsequently be directed to
representatives of outside groups, particularly antiwar organizations after the original distribution. This
distribution would contain an attached anonymous note,
which would read:

"Understand this had wide circulation
among Trotskyites. Have you seen it?"

It is felt the original distribution to selected
party members be mailed from the Boston, Mass., Chicago,
Ill., and San Francisco, California, areas where no
particular party factions exist, however, areas which
embrace a considerable number of party members. This would
preclude immediate blame on any particular party member
or group and lend credence to the possession of addresses
of party members in these geographical areas. The
subsequent mailing to anti-war committees and opposing
radical groups would then be mailed 4 days hence from
NYC. It is felt that many individuals from the NYC
area would have access to addresses of these organizations
on a national basis.

Within 10 days, the receiving offices are
requested to furnish the NYO the names and addresses
of approximately 20 per cent of the membership of the
respective SWP membership, including those who have
expressed some degree of past dissatisfaction with party
policy.

132

Receiving offices are also requested to furnish the NYO the names and addresses of local or national anti-war committees that exist within their respective territories.

One copy of a sample of the anonymous letter is attached for receiving offices. If Bureau authority is granted to implement this suggestion, the anonymous letter will be mimeographed and prepared on commercial paper. The letter and addressed envelopes will then be afforded the Boston, Chicago and Los Angeles Offices for mailings from locations which would not bring suspicion to the Bureau.

It is believed that the above action will definitely create disruption within the ranks of the SWP, particulary on local levels and eventually cause considerable unrest in National Headquarters. Moreover, this action should seriously hamper the party's total occupation at this time, that is, its anti-war actions and objectives.

"AN OPEN LETTER TO TROTSKYITES"

You're a Trotskyite.

You've struggled through the years attempting to influence others with your particular line of revolutionary socialism. You've seen your Party's membership cut time and time again by a seemingly endless series of splits, to the point where, historically, the SWP has become known as the "party of splits".

During the late 1950's, you entered, with your party, into a regroupment effort with dissident ex-CPers who were disillusioned over the crushing of the Hungarian Revolution and the Khrushchev Revelations of the 20th Congress of the CPSU. You watched as your party shunned the true principles of regroupment on a common ground and unsuccessfully attempted to dominate and recruit, thus gaining the reputation as "spoilers".

You then picked up your chipped marbles and plunged into the support of the Cuban Revolution by taking dead aim on the Fair Play For Cuba Committee. Your party succeeded in placing its "professional secretary", Berta Green, into the FPCC leadership. You didn't have to wait long, however, before your party's "raiding" operation within the FPCC on a national basis became evident. So, it wasn't too much of a surprise when Berta was bounced from the FPCC and your party once again was accused of a crude attempt to "take over" rather than provide constructive assistance to a most worthy cause.

Far from dismayed, you next created the "independent" Committee To Aid The Monroe Defendants, with the expectations of reaching the Negro with the party line. Naturally, you placed Berta Green, now available, as secretary of this committee. Your party then proceeded, under the cloak of pseudo-respectability, to implement its ultimate aims of domination and recruitment. This activity necessitated considerable effort on your part, but eventually incurred nothing but the wrath of honest independents. To make it worse, you had to absorb the responsibility for the loss of funds and the creation of actual public harm to these victims in Monroe, North Carolina ----- to the end that you were made to suffer public attack and disavowal by no less than the defendants themselves. A most disheartening episode on behalf of the oppressed victims of the racist state, but still, the SWP was the only existing Trotskyist party, wasn't it? So you hung on.

The FBI's elaborate efforts to discredit the SWP's role in the Monroe committee, referred to in this "open letter," are documented in chapters 4 and 7. Berta Green (now

In recent years, your party has taken a page from the book of Stalin by its purges of party members who have attempted to present for discussion alternative viewpoints of current situations. Thus, your party was responsible, in effect, for the creation of additional splinter groups including the "Spartacist" movement which has attained considerable renown in the radical community.

Presently, you've been struggling with your party in its efforts to become part of the greatest ground swell of opposition to this country's imperialist policies that has ever existed. To this end, you had high hopes as the party's youth arm, the Young Socialist Alliance, was dispatched to Washington, D. C. last Thanksgiving to participate in anti-war conferences and a massive demonstration of protest to U. S. intervention in Vietnam. Surely, this was an unprecedented opportunity to militate against Washington and Wall Street. But, true to the SWP's history of sectarianism, you witnessed the young "Trots" promote a divisionary and undermining line of "immediate withdrawal" at these conferences.

Prophetically, you saw your party and its youth soundly defeated at this conference in yet another attempt to recruit through division and domination. Your attempt to "save face", following this debacle, was the promotion of a Caucus of "independent" anti-war committees based solely on immediate withdrawal of U. S. forces in Vietnam. And you justly suspect now that this tactic is viewed by radicals and independents alike as a "paper front" composed of committees hastily formed and led by YSA members throughout the country. The people publishing and contributing to "The Newsletter" of this Caucus only too well confirm this fact.

Your ultimate dismay was recently realized when your party and its movement was bitterly attacked by Fidel Castro as "splitters and agents of imperialism". Thus, you have been made to suffer the final irony. Your party, which has posed as one of the leading defenders of the Cuban Revolution, now finds itself in the most ironic position of defending itself from a scathing attack by Castro himself!

Such is the state of affairs and mind in which you now find yourself ----- sick with the realization that your party and its youth have finally achieved utter disrespect by all those whom it has strived to influence.

Your humiliation in the public and radical press is now complete as you sadly observe your FORMER party press on.

Berta Langston) is an SWP member who helped initiate defense efforts for the Cuban revolution and the Monroe defendants.

135

UNITED STATES GOVERNMENT

Memorandum

TO : DIRECTOR, FBI ⬛⬛⬛   DATE: 8/30/66

FROM : SAC, NEW YORK ⬛⬛⬛

SUBJECT: SWP
IS-SWP
DISRUPTION PROGRAM

ReNYlet to Director 7/6/66.

The reported reactions of the SWP and actions taken as reported to date, regarding the anonymous mailings referred to in relet have been afforded the Bureau.

During recent months the SWP, particularly in the NYC area, has noticeably decreased its emphasis on activity within local anti-war committees. Party emphasis in this regard at this time amounts to the placing of one comrade in each committee in the event something of interest to the Party occurs in regard to any one of these committees. This slackening of emphasis in the placing of many comrades in these committees has not been explained to the general Party membership to date.

In a recent confidential memorandum prepared by the Political Committee of the SWP, the Party referred to a condition of dichotomy as existing within the various anti-war committees and organizations and considered itself as the left organization participating in these committees. It is felt, therefore, that the Party has experienced considerable difficulty in achieving its aims and objectives within these committees which may in part have resulted from information furnished these committees through the anonymous mailings.

It is further noted that a Party leader recently stated that the SWP must, under all circumstances, not "antagonize" any elements in the anti-war movement inasmuch as the Party "has always been accused of splitting", which accusation greatly upsets the Party. In this regard the above confidential memorandum also sets forth that the Party should make certain concessions with other radical organizations in order that they will not be accused of diversionary tactics. This is considered by the Party as its "new political tactic" In view of the above, it is felt that the Party's influence and prestige within the anti-war movement is of a tenuous nature at this time.

Buy U.S. Savings Bonds ... on the Payroll Savings Plan

136

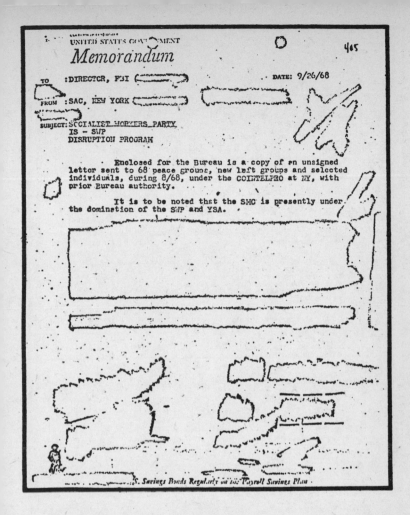

UNITED STATES GOVERNMENT

Memorandum

TO : DIRECTOR, FBI

FROM : SAC, NEW YORK

DATE: 9/26/68

SUBJECT: SOCIALIST WORKERS PARTY
IS - SWP
DISRUPTION PROGRAM

Enclosed for the Bureau is a copy of an unsigned letter sent to 68 peace groups, new left groups and selected individuals, during 8/68, under the COINTELPRO at NY, with prior Bureau authority.

It is to be noted that the SMC is presently under the domination of the SWP and YSA.

S. Savings Bonds Regularly on the Payroll Savings Plan

Pages 137 and 138: One of the FBI's many efforts to split and derail the antiwar movement was this 1968 red-baiting attack on the Young Socialist Alliance. The anonymous letter singles out the YSA's advocacy of street demonstrations, encouraging the idea that these made "zero contributions to the ending of the Johnson war."

137

WHO BUSTED SMC'S ASS?

Events since the disaster on June 29-30, have again demonstrated that everything the YSA touches turns to pure horseshit. Kipp Dawson and her gang of hypocrites took poor old SMC apart, changed all the pieces around, and put it back in the form of a sterile YSA group. Useless talk and parliamentary procedure is the new name of the game.

We who had served SMC from the begining shed a few bitter tears, packed our bags and left. Linda Morse had the vision too. She saw through the Trotskyite shit and followed her nose through the door. She wasn't alone either. Many others, including Resistance, WRL, SDS and the Du Bois Clubs, followed her into the clear. So, we formed the Radical Organizing Committee to deal with issues related to the dirty war in Vietnam, the draft, racism and campus complicity. We wonder how long it will be before YSA takes a bead on the ROC?

We admit to a few hangups - mostly financial - but the Trotskyites have had many for years. There's the street-meeting hangup. We suspect that any SMC activity in the future will be in the form of YSA street meetings - zero contributions to the ending of the Johnson war. While the Trotskyites talk and talk, the war goes on and on.

All of which builds to a fine point - known to most of the independents in SMC for a long time. The old-line organizations have completely dried up.....nothing but dust between the ears. Let's face it, the contributions of the SWP, YSA and PL to the movement have been minimal to say the least. The CP died of old age several decades ago, although we understand Gus is living real well.

We think ROC has something new to offer - a new approach to the problems of our times, a new light on the rise of radical consciousness within the student movement. This time, baby, the fascist taptics of the YSA are not going to get the chance to wreck the organization. No more committee packing and other high handed crap so neatly done by the Trotskyites. YSA can stick with its own hangups. We don't want 'em!

With it all, you have to admire the way YSA operated. Kipp and Syd were beautiful....just beautiful. They stuffed their platform up our collective asses smiling all the while. They were pained when we left. Kipp still looks pained.

We'll work for ROC now. Let's see what happens. A final word for YSA. "You busted our ass. You and you alone. Good luck mothers."

— Peace

RECEIVED FROM

SEP 5 1975

FBI

CI .100-17601

Antioch prides itself greatly on a "highly intellectual", and "academic, scholarly environment."

Actually the campus is most often run by a small group of militants that are permitted by college authorities to attack every segment of American society under the semblance of being "highly intellectual."

Anyone visiting the campus doubts its "academic, scholarly environment" because of the dirty anti-social appearance, and behavior of a large number of students can be seen to have the fullest "beatnik image."

Yellow Springs follows the lead of Antioch. It has an overabundance of self-declared "intellectuals," whose morals and habits are also anti-social.

The college and Yellow Springs have been virtually sealed off from scrutiny by others. Students demonstrate, and the college newspaper protests the appearance on campus of a representative of any investigative agency or military agency. Local newspaper editorializes against any logical support or police agencies.

RECOMMENDATION:

Cincinnati recommends that Counterintelligence action be taken to expose the pseudo intellectual image of Antioch by the following:

1. Review files at Cincinnati to identify 30 to 40 former students who were militant campus leaders.

2. Set out leads to other offices to discreetly determine the achievement of these individuals since leaving Antioch.

3. Continuing this method, identify a significant number who have attended Antioch, and have a low achievement record as shown by public source material.

4. Furnish results to ~~████████████~~, ~~████████~~ ~~████████████████~~ "Cincinnati Enquirer," a newspaper of

---

Pages 139–140: J. Edgar Hoover authorized the Cincinnati field office to launch a campaign "to force Antioch to defend itself as an educational institution" and to pressure the college administration to end campus protest activity. The FBI complained that students, faculty, and townspeople had protested on-campus military and intelligence recruiting and activities of the "police agencies," including the FBI itself.

CI 100-17601

general circulation at Cincinnati, Ohio. ⎯⎯⎯ is also an
SAC contact. Agreement would be made with ⎯⎯⎯ to use this
material in n article questioning whether Antioch is in fact
"highly inte .lectual" and whether students are actually
receiving a quality education there.

⎯⎯⎯ Following publishing of the ⎯⎯⎯ article, give
wide anonym us circulation of copies to parents of current
students identified from student directories. Also circulate
copies of the article to members of the Board of Directors of
Antioch and to the personnel directors of all businesses that
are a part of the Antioch co-op plan.

DESIRED RESULT OF ACTION:

Force Antioch to defend itself as an educational
institution. Force attention on activities on the Antioch
campus by the parents who are sending their children to the
college for an education. Force the Antioch administrators to
curtail the activities of those students who spend most of their
time engaging in anti-social activity, protest demonstrations,
and affiliation with subversive groups.

Cincinnati will take no action on this recommendation
until it has been reviewed at the Bureau, and authorization is
received.

Vol. I, #2 Indiana University, Bloomington, Indiana 10/25/68

PURPOSE

As set out in our first "Armageddon News" issue, we students are concerned for the need for truth within our antiwar movement at Indiana University. As students, we feel the war in Vietnam is a political and military travesty, foisted on the American people by an unsympathetic administration, an administration unmindful of the will of the people. This situation, we can, and should deal with at the polls. The truth of the situation here at IU, however, is that this dissatisfaction with national policy is being used by a few to seize the university and to strike at the heart of the democratic system. We will simply point out the truth of this situation and you be the judge.

The Committee to End the War in Vietnam (CEWV)

Last year, members of the CEWV made an attempt to take over an academic building at IU, assaulting the police and violating the law in the process. They apparently thought that they were "different" and "above the law." This group felt free to use illegal methods to achieve their end. The big question now is just what was that end? Of the 35 arrested, all were convicted.

Last semester, Russell Block and Mark Ritchey set up a puppet by the name of Eric Shepard to act as Chairman of the CEWV. If you will look closely, you will find that Block and Ritchey, both members of the Young Socialist Alliance, pulled the strings for Shepard to jump. These people are the "manipulators" at IU and have the greatest influence on the "New Left" through the CEWV.

Last semester, Block and Ritchey announced the CEWV sponsorship of a series of lectures on "Socialism" and "The Communist Manifesto." These lectures were given, in part,

Pages 141 and 142: The second issue of Armageddon News, *published and distributed secretly by the FBI for two semesters at Indiana University in Bloomington. It purported to be the work of antiwar students "concerned for the need for truth," but its right-wing slanders had no effect on genuine students opposed to the war.*

141

by an officer of the Young Socialist Alliance, Ralph Levitt, a former IU student. Levitt is now the State Chairman of the Socialist Workers Party's campaign and is presently running for Senator on the Socialist Workers Party ticket in the State of Indiana. What we want to know is what relationship do the topics "Socialism" and "The Communist Manifesto" have to do with a free people's rights and attempts to protest the policy of their government.

If this is the way the CEWV is to act, let's not be duped by its name. It's no longer a committee to end the war in Vietnam, no longer a forum for just dissent. It's a recruiting ground for subversion.

We all want an end to this war and we have a right to protest our government's participation therein. Ask yourself, then, what can be the true purpose of those who want to use your name and your energy for their objectives. It's surely worth your time and your effort to inquire penetratingly into organizations and causes that entreat your support.

A case in point is that the campus newspaper on 9/24/68 reported that CEWV is making plans to support the "International Days of Solidarity," planned by the Student Mobilization Committee (SMC) for the week of 10/21/68, and a large antiwar demonstration planned at IU for 10/26/68. Let's find out who we are declaring ourselves in solidarity with and what this Student Mobilization Committee really is. It wouldn't be surprising to find a considerable covey of SWP'ers behind it.

"DON'T LET THE NEW LEFT WIN THE ARMAGEDDON AT IU"

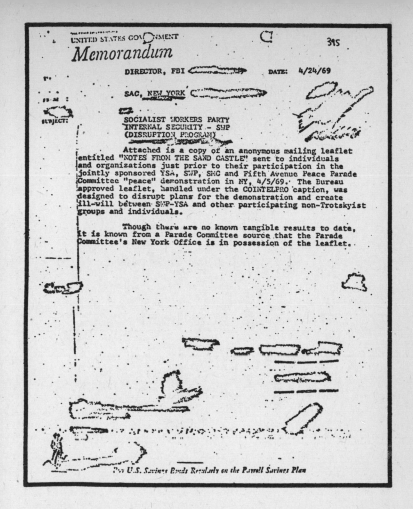

Memorandum

395

DIRECTOR, FBI ⟨⟩   DATE: 4/24/69

TO:

SAC, NEW YORK ⟨⟩

FROM:

SUBJECT: SOCIALIST WORKERS PARTY
             INTERNAL SECURITY - SWP
             (DISRUPTION PROGRAM)

             Attached is a copy of an anonymous mailing leaflet
entitled "NOTES FROM THE SAND CASTLE" sent to individuals
and organizations just prior to their participation in the
jointly sponsored YSA, SWP, SMC and Fifth Avenue Peace Parade
Committee "peace" demonstration in NY, 4/5/69. The Bureau
approved leaflet, handled under the COINTELPRO caption, was
designed to disrupt plans for the demonstration and create
ill-will between SWP-YSA and other participating non-Trotskyist
groups and individuals.

             Though there are no known tangible results to date,
it is known from a Parade Committee source that the Parade
Committee's New York Office is in possession of the leaflet.

Buy U.S. Savings Bonds Regularly on the Payroll Savings Plan

Pages 143 and 144: This 1969 FBI operation was designed to "disrupt plans for the demonstration and create ill-will" by red-baiting and ridiculing mass marches. The last paragraph of the "newsletter" in particular advocates violent confrontations with police.

<u>ITEM</u>: Mark well the date April 5th, kiddies. That's the day our old pals in the YSA-SWP-SMC coalition fall flat on their hard-worn asses. Any demonstration planned by the young Socialist Alliance is bad enough, but when they are joined by their fellow finks in the Student Mobe and Socialist Workers, we develop a strong urge to vomit into the wind. In any event, April 5th promises to be a genuine "peace dud" to be salted away with the YSA collection of duds. Our fair city may be waist high in dog shit now, but on April 6th you'll be swimming in bull shit.

<u>ITEM</u>: Speaking of April 6th, the original plans of SWP-YSA called for the "peace march" to be held on that date - the same date on which the Christian world celebrates Easter. The master plan was presented to the Fifth Avenue Peace Parade Committee by Rick Wadsworth, Joanna Misnick and several other "kids" a few weeks ago. Stout hearts on the Committee turned to jelly when they visualized movement people being massacred by irate Christians dressed in Easter finery. "Let's make it April 5th", whined Fifth Avenue. "We don't want the plastic society too pissed off!" That was that. Wow!

<u>ITEM</u>: Chicago's "Vietnam GI" takes a rather dim view of the whole bit. Their opposition is natural when you figure the YSA'ers are trying to take the starch out of the GI movement. Other organizations have split from the April 5th extravaganza which, like most SWP operations, was formulated and put into motion with no consideration for other groups which might be interested. Take SDS for example. We're doing our thing April 12th. Even shaky Dave Dellinger is lending vocal support to the SDS scene. Don't look for us on the 5th, pals.

<u>ITEM</u>: The truth of the matter is that the SWP-YSA-SMC coalition has never had the guts to play it like it really is. They march to confront the establishment and find the landscape crawling with pigs. Since you can't sell the "Militant" to pigs, they cut and run. You'll never see Matilda Zimmerman with battle wounds, chums.

             - Peace

             Bernie
             (Sand Castle Class of '71)

UNITED STATES GOVERNMENT

Memorandum

TO : DIRECTOR, FBI

DATE: 1/21/70

FROM : SAC, ATLANTA

SUBJECT: COINTELPRO - NEW LEFT
IS

During the past several months, Socialist Workers
Party/Young Socialist Alliance and Atlanta Revolutionary
Youth Movement/Students for a Democratic Society have been
so uncooperative as the two largest factions in a "coalition"
of Atlanta New Left and pacifist groups banded together
to make a bigger and better local showing in anti-war
demonstrations, that most of the demonstrations have been
unsuccessful and disappointing to participants. "The
Great Speckled Bird", Atlanta's New Left newspaper, has
run several articles during the past six months which
referred to "coalition" meetings as "pitiful meetings,"
pointing out that the "stupid bickering "between the two
factions made the group" a "paper coalition " of "extremely
limited usefulness." This situation was instrumental in
keeping the morale in Atlanta's anti-war movement at a low
ebb, as evidenced by the fact that an estimated 125 persons
from the entire area participated in the anti-war demonstration
in Washington, D. C., on 11/15/69, after much effort by
the "coalition", which had originally chartered nine buses
to carry participants and was talking about having as
many as 1000 people in Washington.

However, since ARYM/SDS allegedly dropped their
affiliation with SDS in late November, 1969, and became merely
"RYM", they have allegedly apologized to the "coalition"
for their uncooperative attitude in the past and have
indicated a willingness to cooperate with the "coalition"
in local anti-war activities. This was apparently evidenced
in an Atlanta anti-war conference held on 1/17/70, at
which RYM was well represented, and DAVID SIMPSON of the
RYM leaders, was appointed as Co-coordinator of a forthcoming
anti-war type demonstration to be held in Atlanta during

Buy U.S. Savings Bonds Regularly on the Payroll Savings Plan

the anticipated visit of Vice President SPIRO AGNEW on
2/21/70, after SIMPSON had been defeated by a YSA member
in an election for the position, his appointment as
Co-coordinator being then suggested by a local SWP/YSA
leader.

It would appear that it would be greatly
to the Bureau's advantage not to let these two major
factions in the Atlanta anti-war movement become overly
friendly and cooperative. It is, therefore, suggested
that the Bureau authorize the mailing of the following
anonymous letter to DAVID SIMPSON:

"Dear Dave,

"How can you RYM people be so naive and
gullible as to continue to let the Trots run
the whole show their way as they did again at
the anti-war conference at Emory. It looks
like you could see that they have the whole
thing figured out, and have all the answers
before these so-called "conferences" even
start.

"As a communist, which they say you are,
you sure don't show any knowledge of communist
tactics. Why don't you check out your Trot
friends on the night before your "conference,"
and you might find that they are together,
busy with plans as to how they will manipulate
the coalition to their own specifications --
being gracious enough to throw you a few
scraps to keep you happy.

"Our revolution is a long way off if
we have to wait for them to do it their way--
they've been carrying the ball for years, now
it should be someone else's turn.

                    "A Friend "

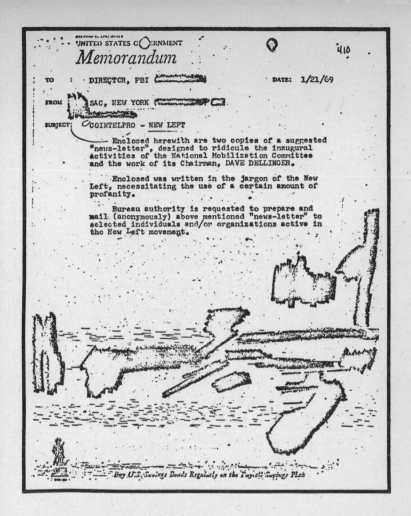

TO : DIRECTOR, FBI

DATE: 1/21/69

FROM : SAC, NEW YORK

SUBJECT: COINTELPRO - NEW LEFT

Enclosed herewith are two copies of a suggested "news-letter", designed to ridicule the inaugural activities of the National Mobilization Committee and the work of its Chairman, DAVE DELLINGER.

Enclosed was written in the jargon of the New Left, necessitating the use of a certain amount of profanity.

Bureau authority is requested to prepare and mail (anonymously) above mentioned "news-letter" to selected individuals and/or organizations active in the New Left movement.

Buy U.S. Savings Bonds Regularly on the Payroll Savings Plan

Pages 147 and 148: This anonymous mailing, in addition to personal ridicule of antiwar leader Dave Dellinger, attempted to spread suspicion over the use of movement funds and create friction between MOBE and SDS.

FLASH   FLASH   FLASH   FLASH   FLASH   FLASH

DESPERATE DAVE DANGLES DINGUS

Murderously Mangles MOBE

Washington, D. C. Jan. 20 - Speaking in his usual high pitched
voice, Dave Dellinger, National Chairman of the National
Mobilization Committee (MOBE), today claimed that the anti-
inaugural demonstrations called by his organization had been
responsible in getting the Paris peace talks going again.

Dellinger made this startling disclosure before an audience
of newsmen in the dingy Hawthorne School which housed many
of his followers. A cluster of the latter stood behind their
Guru sniffling and fingering wilted flowers. Dellinger,
looking pale - more fairy-like than ever - tried to control
the squeaks in his voice to no avail. "How many demonstrators
did MOBE bring to the inaugural?", he was asked.

"At least 10,000," he answered.

"Bullshit", was heard in several sections of the room.

Dellinger shuffled his notes. "Let's make that 5,000."

"Bullshit".

"Would you believe 3,000?" Silence. Dave rolled his eyes
at the ceiling. "I'm not going to play at numbers," he chirped.
"What matters is that MOBE accomplished so much. We did get the
peace talks going. We did break some windows in the National
Geographic Society building. Despite police brutality, our
brave people managed to throw cans and sticks at the President."
His voice went higher - sounding like glass bells in a soft
summer breeze. "We shook the establishment, gentlemen."

Associated Press stood up. "We understand MOBE is broke. Tha
you lost control of the thing. That SDS and many other
organizations in the peace movement refused to back you. That
you have no idea how MOBE funds were spent."

Dellinger put a finger in his mouth and sucked it
reflectively. Some minutes passed before he spoke. "MOBE
is solvent, boys. As of this morning, we have $1.54 in the
treasury. The price of peace is high." He tried to look grim.
"SDS, of course, is just a bunch of dirty college kids with grass
for brains. We didn't want them or need them. He formed his
lips into a cute bow. "I must go now. We're hitching a ride
back to New York today unless we can raise bus fare."

He shoved four fingers into his mouth and was led slowly
from the room humming "We Shall Overcome."

7 Red-baiting

In the last chapter we saw some examples of the FBI's use of red-baiting in the antiwar movement—smearing its targets as "subversives," "manipulators," or whatever else might appeal to the prejudices of the intended audience.

The different varieties of this technique are such a mainstay of FBI sabotage that it is worth studying them in somewhat more detail.

The FBI uses red-baiting in two ways. The first is more familiar, and we have already seen some examples. Information is fed to newspaper columnists and politicians who are sympathetic to the FBI. For example, during the movement against the war in Vietnam, on the eve of a demonstration, some columnist or newspaper would suddenly "reveal" that socialists were active in organizing the demonstration.

The purpose would be to create the impression that socialists were secretly controlling the action for their own ulterior motives. This was intended to scare people away from coming out to oppose the war. The Cointelpro papers contain examples of the FBI's use of the news media in this way.

The documents reproduced in this chapter show the other way the FBI employs red-baiting. The message and the objective are the same. The difference is that the red-baiting seems to be coming from supporters of the Black, antiwar, or labor movements.

The FBI tries to initiate or encourage the exclusion of socialists, who are depicted as dishonest individuals who lack a sincere concern for the movement and are not to be trusted.

The FBI's aim is to turn people away from fighting their enemy and toward fighting each other.

Why did the FBI think it could get results with these methods? The reason is that anticommunist prejudices run very deep in this society.

These prejudices have their roots in the anticommunist hysteria which began in the late 1940s and continued, although weakened, into the 1960s. The anticommunist witch-hunt coincided with the cold war between the United States and the Soviet Union. Americans were taught that communism was evil incarnate and that godless communists were out to rule the world. This was necessary to convince the American people to support massive war expenditures, go along with wars like those in Korea and Vietnam, and maintain a huge standing army to act as world policeman for capitalism.

At home, this campaign meant that socialists and communists had to be driven out of public life. Venal politicians—like Nixon—built political careers on the anticommunist issue.

Members of the Socialist Workers party, the Communist party, and other radical groups were thrown out of government jobs and out of the union movement. Pressure was put on Black organizations to exclude socialists from their ranks.

Hollywood churned out productions depicting Marxists as soulless agents of an alien force out to destroy America. If socialists or communists appeared to be working for some good cause, this was merely a clever trick to disguise their true aims and to win unsuspecting converts. A whole generation was weaned on this.

But the rise of the Black civil rights movement beginning in late fifties and the mass antiwar movement of the sixties changed a lot of things.

The rulers began to find that the "Communist menace" was no longer sufficient to rouse Americans to die in Southeast Asia. Opponents of the Vietnam War learned that it was impossible to build a movement against a war that was justified by anticommunism while making concessions to anticommunist ideology within the movement itself. The principle of nonexclusion was established in the antiwar movement. Anyone could participate— be they Democrat, Republican, Communist, or Socialist—as long as they agreed with the goal of ending the war.

Much to the dismay of the FBI, the old-style anticommunism of the 1950s lacked the power to destroy the antiwar movement. Columnists Rowland Evans and Robert Novak could write on the eve of the April 24, 1971, antiwar demonstration that Socialist Workers party leader Fred Halstead was one of the central organizers of the action and have virtually no impact on the million people who turned out in Washington, D.C., and San Francisco.

While this type of red-baiting was becoming less and less useful, the FBI focused increasing attention on Red-baiting that was made to appear as if it came from within the movement.

One of the reasons the FBI found this tactic so useful is that, unfortunately, some forces inside the movement engage in red-baiting as a substitute for political discussion.

This sometimes takes the form of charges that the SWP and YSA are "opportunist." What people who make this accusation are insinuating is that socialists are not really interested in furthering, for example, the antiracist struggle but are merely "using" it for some unspecified selfish end.

Red-baiting is almost invariably used in order to avoid or obscure a discussion of real political differences. A relatively recent example occurred at the February 14-16, 1975, antiracist conference in Boston. Some 2,000 people from across the country gathered to found a new organization, the National Student Coalition Against Racism. After a weekend of democratic discussion and debate, NSCAR voted overwhelmingly to help build the national march on Boston called by the NAACP to support busing and desegregation of Boston schools. Some 15,000 people marched in Boston the following May 17.

A group led by members of some Maoist sects tried to disrupt the conference by charging that the whole affair was "dominated," "manipulated," and "controlled behind the scenes" by the "opportunists" of the YSA and SWP.

The disrupters delayed the conference for a while and finally decided to walk out. As they were leaving they said, "We demand an end to busing, an end to federal troops, and an end to this whole fucked-up reactionary conference!"

Then it became clear for all to see that their red-baiting slanders were simply a cover for their political opposition to a movement in defense of busing, which was the entire purpose of the desegregation conference.

Differences of opinion will arise in any healthy, living movement, and discussion of those political differences can only help make the movement stronger. Red-baiting poisons the atmosphere and makes discussion impossible. It sows the seeds of suspicion and distrust.

The FBI is well aware of this. These documents provide some important lessons. They show who benefits from red-baiting—the

FBI, the racists, and the reactionaries. And they show who loses—the labor movement, the civil rights movement, and other movements for social change.

The documents on the following pages are concerned with five different Cointelpro operations. Four involve the use of red-baiting to disrupt the antiwar movement and the Black civil rights movement. The fifth operation was designed to intensify hostility between the Socialist Workers party and the Communist party.

• The first set of documents includes an obscene, sexist leaflet, purportedly issued by an opponent of the war in Vietnam. This leaflet was mailed to a large number of antiwar activists. It calls for excluding the Young Socialist Alliance and the Socialist Workers party from the national antiwar coalition.

Its purpose, in the FBI's words, was "to cause disruption in the peace movement, primarily in the New Mobilization Committee to End the War in Vietnam, and to minimize the growing influence of the SWP in the movement."

• The next selection from the FBI files involves an attempt to cause the NAACP to withdraw its endorsement of the Committee to Aid the Monroe Defendants (CAMD) in 1962. (Another operation against the CAMD is described in chapter 4.)

The national NAACP had not endorsed the CAMD, but some local chapters had. The FBI mailed an anonymous letter to NAACP Executive Secretary Roy Wilkins falsely charging that the CAMD "was set up, dominated, and controlled by the Socialist Workers Party." The letter insinuated, without offering a shred of evidence, that CAMD funds were being misused by the SWP.

• The third set of documents concerns the campaign of Sam Jordan, a Black candidate for mayor of San Francisco in 1963. He ran independently of the Democratic party, and the SWP extended support to his campaign. The FBI mailed an unsigned letter that, in their words, was "ostensibly from a longshoreman who wants to vote for Jordan because of Jordan's strong stand for Negro rights but the writer is concerned because of all the known Socialist Workers Party (SWP) members who are running Jordan's campaign."

• Fourth is an anonymous "memorandum" from "a member" of the National Steering Committee of the New Mobilization Committee, an antiwar coalition The "memo" charges that the "Trotskyites . . . have seen fit to use the good offices of the NMC to further their own political aspirations, nebulous as they are."

• Finally, there is a 1962 directive from FBI headquarters in Washington to its New York office instructing them to try to stir up friction between the SWP and the Communist party. The *Worker*, the newspaper reflecting the views of the Communist party at that time, had recently run an advertisement containing the address of the New York SWP offices as a location to purchase tickets for a benefit for the Irish movement. The FBI telephoned the *Militant* and the *Worker* in order to provoke animosity around this ad. It is interesting to note, in the FBI's evaluation of this operation, that the *Militant* editor did not rise to the bait.

These documents do not, it should be remembered, tell the whole story. The FBI is refusing to turn over many of its files. We can assume that some of them contain information about more recent Cointelpro operations, such as those directed against the women's movement.

Also, the FBI is refusing to release any documents or sections of documents that it claims reveal "investigative techniques." "Investigative techniques," we know, include bugging, wiretapping, mail tampering, and burglaries. The present documents have been censored to remove these unsavory aspects of FBI work. It is also well known that the FBI uses its undercover agents in various movements to encourage violence, disunity, and red-baiting attacks.

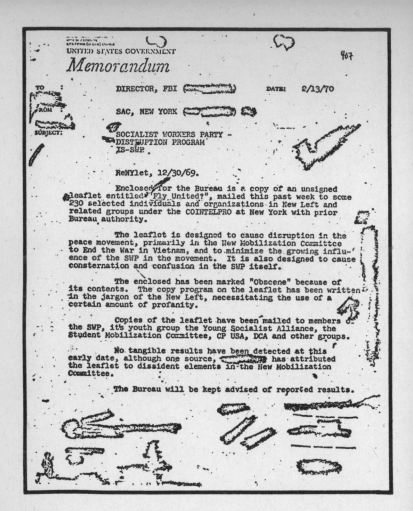

UNITED STATES GOVERNMENT

467

Memorandum

TO : DIRECTOR, FBI ▓▓▓▓▓▓▓▓▓ DATE: 2/13/70

FROM : SAC, NEW YORK ▓▓▓▓▓ ▓▓

SUBJECT: SOCIALIST WORKERS PARTY –
DISRUPTION PROGRAM
IS-SWP

ReNYlet, 12/30/69.

Enclosed for the Bureau is a copy of an unsigned leaflet entitled "Fly United?", mailed this past week to some 230 selected individuals and organizations in New Left and related groups under the COINTELPRO at New York with prior Bureau authority.

The leaflet is designed to cause disruption in the peace movement, primarily in the New Mobilization Committee to End the War in Vietnam, and to minimize the growing influence of the SWP in the movement. It is also designed to cause consternation and confusion in the SWP itself.

The enclosed has been marked "Obscene" because of its contents. The copy program on the leaflet has been written in the jargon of the New Left, necessitating the use of a certain amount of profanity.

Copies of the leaflet have been mailed to members of the SWP, its youth group the Young Socialist Alliance, the Student Mobilization Committee, CP USA, DCA and other groups.

No tangible results have been detected at this early date, although one source, ▓▓▓▓▓▓ has attributed the leaflet to dissident elements in the New Mobilization Committee.

The Bureau will be kept advised of reported results.

Pages 154 and 155: In 1970 the FBI mailed a red-baiting leaflet, ostensibly from an antiwar activist, to "cause

FLY UNITED?

BALLS!

Dig it. It's time to pull the chain, brothers and sisters. If the peace movement in Amerika is to survive, the crap influence of the Socialist Workers Party and its bastard youth group - Young Socialist Alliance - must be flushed from New Mobe once and for all. Stagnant zeros like Freddie Halstead and Harry Ring, both members of the SWP Nat'l Committee, must be dumped. Let's get rid of the Carol Lipmans, Gus Horowitzs and the Joanna Misniks along with other SWP shits! DEMAND AN END TO SWP BALLING! Write New Mobe today at Suite 900, 1029 Vermont Ave., N.W., Washington, D.C.

Write today!

disruption in the peace movement . . . and to minimize the growing influence of the SWP."

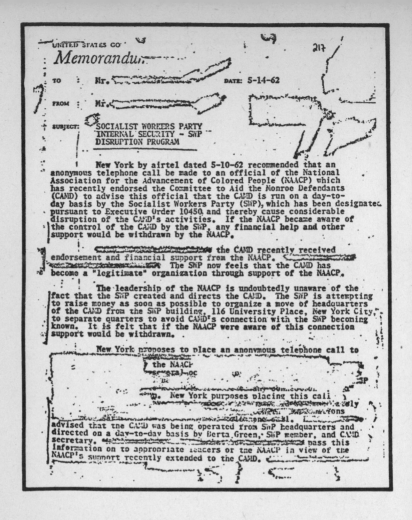

UNITED STATES GO

Memorandum

TO : Mr.   DATE: 5-14-62

FROM : Mr.

SUBJECT: SOCIALIST WORKERS PARTY
INTERNAL SECURITY - SWP
DISRUPTION PROGRAM

New York by airtel dated 5-10-62 recommended that an anonymous telephone call be made to an official of the National Association for the Advancement of Colored People (NAACP) which has recently endorsed the Committee to Aid the Monroe Defendants (CAMD) to advise this official that the CAMD is run on a day-to-day basis by the Socialist Workers Party (SWP), which has been designated pursuant to Executive Order 10450 and thereby cause considerable disruption of the CAMD's activities. If the NAACP became aware of the control of the CAMD by the SWP, any financial help and other support would be withdrawn by the NAACP.

the CAMD recently received endorsement and financial support from the NAACP. The SWP now feels that the CAMD has become a "legitimate" organization through support of the NAACP.

The leadership of the NAACP is undoubtedly unaware of the fact that the SWP created and directs the CAMD. The SWP is attempting to raise money as soon as possible to organize a move of headquarters of the CAMD from the SWP building, 116 University Place, New York City, to separate quarters to avoid CAMD's connection with the SWP becoming known. It is felt that if the NAACP were aware of this connection support would be withdrawn.

New York proposes to place an anonymous telephone call to
the NAACP
secretary oc

New York purposes placing this call
ions
advised that the CAMD was being operated from SWP headquarters and directed on a day-to-day basis by Berta Green, SWP member, and CAMD secretary. pass this information on to appropriate leaders of the NAACP in view of the NAACP's support recently extended to the CAMD.

Pages 156–162: A 1962 operation aimed at destroying the Committee to Aid the Monroe Defendants by claiming it was secretly controlled by the SWP for ulterior purposes. Washington approved New York's plan for an anonymous

Memorandum to
RE: SOCIALIST WORKERS PARTY

this information would be verified by a visit to SWP headquarters, 116 University Place, New York City.

The SWP intends to use this committee to make a national and international issue out of charges lodged against Robert Franklin Williams and other individuals who were involved in a racial incident during demonstration: held at Monroe, North Carolina, on 8-27-61. Williams was charged with interstate flight to avoid prosecution on charges of kidnapping a white couple at gunpoint and is reportedly in Cuba. The SWP has been organizing branches of the CAMD throughout the United States where branches of the SWP exist.

It is felt that this operation should be approved since the possible withdrawal of NAACP support would have considerable disruptive effect upon the SWP and cause considerable damage to future SWP activities in the civil rights field.

advised that a letter has been directed to an official of the NAACP containing this informa-tion. Such a letter should be signed as being from a true friend and supporter of Negro rights.

RECOMMENDATION:

That the attached airtel to the New York Office be approved authorizing the disruption program operation as outlined above and instructing New York that a letter had been sent to an NAACP official containing similar information. Precautionary statements are included.

phone call to the NAACP, cynically suggesting that it be coupled with a letter from "a true friend and supporter of Negro rights."

157

May 16, 1962   218

Airtel

To: SAC, New York: ~~~~~

From: Director, ~~~~~

SOCIALIST WORKERS PARTY
INTERNAL SECURITY - SWP
DISRUPTION PROGRAM

Reurairtel 5-10-62.

The Socialist Workers Party (SWP) Disruption Program operation as outlined in reairtel is approved. However, in addition to placing the anonymous telephone call ~~~~~, you should prepare an anonymous letter to an official of the National Association for the Advancement of Colored People in New York containing similar information. In addition, the fact that this letter is being sent should also be mentioned ~~~~~ to insure that proper authorities are advised of the telephone call received by Hill. This letter should be signed a true friend and supporter of Negro rights.

Every precaution should be taken in making the anonymous telephone call ~~~~~ to insure that this call cannot be traced back to the Bureau. In preparing the anonymous letter, commercially purchased stationery should be utilized and it should be addressed in the manner in which mail is usually addressed to the appropriate official.

You should immediately advise the Bureau when this operation has been placed into effect and furnish the Bureau all tangible results promptly.

~~~~~ ON WHICH: See cover memo ~~~~~, dated
~~~~~ caption.

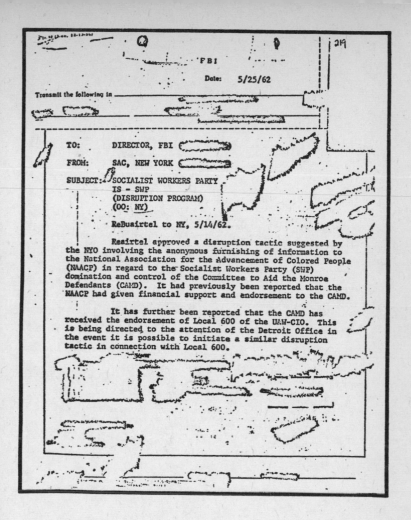

FBI

Date: 5/25/62

Transmit the following in _____

TO: DIRECTOR, FBI

FROM: SAC, NEW YORK

SUBJECT: SOCIALIST WORKERS PARTY
          IS - SWP
          (DISRUPTION PROGRAM)
          (OO: NY)

ReBuairtel to NY, 5/14/62.

Reairtel approved a disruption tactic suggested by the NYO involving the anonymous furnishing of information to the National Association for the Advancement of Colored People (NAACP) in regard to the Socialist Workers Party (SWP) domination and control of the Committee to Aid the Monroe Defendants (CAMD). It had previously been reported that the NAACP had given financial support and endorsement to the CAMD.

It has further been reported that the CAMD has received the endorsement of Local 600 of the UAW-CIO. This is being directed to the attention of the Detroit Office in the event it is possible to initiate a similar disruption tactic in connection with Local 600.

159

AIRTEL TO BUREAU

   Upon receipt of reairtel, efforts were made to contact
   at the NY Headquarters of the NAACP by telephone.

         was reached telephonically
        informed that the caller did not wish
to identify himself, but was distressed at a development in
connection with the NAACP that he had become aware of.
was then told that individuals connected with the CAMD had
said they had obtained the endorsement and support of the
NAACP. was further told that the caller was disappointed
at hearing this because knew that the CAMD operated out of
116 University Place, NYC, and was controlled by the SWP.
denied vigorously that the NAACP had given any backing to the
CAMD.   speaking   of the NAACP,
wished to assure the caller
that the NAACP had not supported the CAMD either openly or
secretly, and that it never would support this organization.

     was told that it was reassuring to hear this, but
it had been widely circulated within the CAMD that backing of
the NAACP had been obtained. The conversation ended with the
caller expressing the hope that was correct and the CAMD
wrong in regard to the statement concerning support because the
caller would hate to think of a fine organization like the NAACP
backing an organization like the CAMD.

       made no statement as to any action he
might take, it was noted that was very forceful in
denial of NAACP connection with the CAMD and anxious to eliminate
any impression the caller had that the NAACP would offer support
in this instance. It is believed quite possible that
may honestly believe that no support has been given and may
check into this matter further. All precautions were taken
to insure that the anonymous telephone call could not
be traced back to the Bureau.

160

As suggested by the Bureau in reairtel, the phone call was followed up by an anonymous letter which was prepared on commercial stationery and mailed at a distance from the FBI Office to Mr. ROY WILKINS, Executive Secretary, NAACP, 20 West 40th Street, NYC. This letter set forth the following:

"Dear Sir:

"An outfit I have some knowledge of, the Committee to Aid the Monroe Defendants, has been boasting lately how they've been made 'legitimate' through the endorsement and financial support of the NAACP.

"No one can deny that the Negro people in Monroe need assistance, but it's a shame that it is tied in with the CAMD.

"You may not have much dealings with the so-called Negro nationalist groups uptown, but many of their leaders could tell you how CAMD was formed.

"It was set up, dominated, and controlled by the Socialist Workers Party, the Trotskyist branch of the communist movement. They use Conrad Lynn as a front man, but CAMD is run by Berta Green, of the SWP. Green was thrown out as secretary of the Fair Play for Cuba Committee to get rid of SWP influence but she bounced right into CAMD. Now the NAACP is supporting what even the FPCC didn't want to be smeared with.

"Ask anyone who has worked with CAMD where the paper work is done, where the mailings are prepared, where a lot of the Monroe contributions are stored. It's the second floor of 116 University Place, which if you don't know, is the SWP hall. Maybe with from NAACP they've been able to move to "a different office by now, but if not, go see for yourself.

"It won't do the work of the NAACP in the South a bit of good if it's known its funds and good name are backing a group in the pocket of the SWP.

"A true friend and supporter of Negro rights"

OPTIONAL FORM NO 10
5010-104

UNITED STATES GOVERNMENT

Memorandum

255

TO: DIRECTOR, FBI

DATE: 10/4/63

FROM: SAC, SAN FRANCISCO

SUBJECT: SOCIALIST WORKERS PARTY
INTERNAL SECURITY - SWP
DISRUPTION PROGRAM

The main activity of the SWP in the San Francisco area at this time is the campaign being conducted by SAM JORDAN for the position of Mayor of San Francisco. The SWP is extremely active on JORDAN's campaign committee and is attempting to inject SWP programs into JORDAN's political campaign. JORDAN is politically naive and has not the slightest idea that the SWP is anything but a group of people interested in helping the Negro better himself. ASHER HARER, a member of the San Francisco Branch of the SWP and of the SWP National Committee, is taking an active part in organizing JORDAN's campaign and is assisted by other SWP members. It is believed that an anonymous letter should be sent to JORDAN pointing out that he is running for Mayor to help his Negro race but is committing political suicide by affiliating himself with communist organizations, such as the SWP. This may cause JORDAN to oust the SWP from his election campaign committee and thereby deny the SWP one avenue through which they are making public the SWP party line.

Authority is therefore requested to send such a letter to JORDAN at his place of business. This would be sent to his place of business, since if it is sent to his headquarters the letter could be opened by someone on his campaign committee, possibly HARER.

Pages 163–166: The FBI's 1963 attempt to have socialists kicked out of an independent Black candidate's campaign committee with a red-baiting letter ostensibly from a longshoreman.

163

UNITED STATES GOVERNMENT

Memorandum

TO : DIRECTOR, FBI

DATE: 10/10/63

FROM : SAC, SAN FRANCISCO

SUBJECT: SOCIALIST WORKERS PARTY
IS - SWP
DISRUPTION PROGRAM

Re Bulet dated 10/8/63.

Set forth below is a proposed anonymous letter to be sent to SAM JORDAN in an effort to force him to oust the SWP from his election campaign committee.

It is to be noted that ASHER HARER, JAMES NICKLAS, HAYDEN PERRY, and CONNIE HANN, who are mentioned in the letter, are members of the San Francisco Branch of the SWP, while AARON CHAPMAN and ALLEN WILLIS are not SWP members. However, WILLIS is a former SWP member and CHAPMAN has long been very close to the SWP and is amenable to SWP control. If JORDAN will oust all of these people from his campaign, the SWP will be shut out from this campaign and it will nullify all of the SWP's recent efforts in San Francisco.

Set forth below is the proposed letter: (Errors in spelling in the letter are intentional)

October ___, 1963
San Francisco, Calif.

Dear Mr. Jordan,

First of all, let me apologise for sending this letter without any name on it, but I am a longshoreman and would not like to have Asher Harer know I am writing this. If he knew he could make things pretty tough for me on the waterfront.

When you indicated that you were running for Mayor of San Francisco to represent negros and other groups who have never been properly represented in San Francisco government I was delighted. However, after attending some of your meetings and noticing who is runing your campaign I have come to the conclusion that you are committing political suicide by allowing people like Harer (a long time wheel in the Socialist Workers Party - the Trotsky communist party) and his stooges Nick Nicklas, Hayden Perry,

164

Connie Hann, Aaron Chapman, and Allen Willis to run your campaign.
By leting them run your campaign you are indicating to the public
that you support communism and that if I support you, then I too
support communism. Now I have no intention of being branded as a
"red" and I know a lot of other people, negro and white, who will
not continue to support you in this election unless you publicly
denounce the SWP and completely cut them out of your campaign.

        You have a big following in San Francisco and could really
do a job in the local political picture. Please don't ruin
everything by allowing yourself to become a tool of the SWP.

                        Sincerely,

                        Disappointed.

P.S. Narer is really using you as a pipe line for the commie line.

165

258

SAC, San Francisco ⟨⟩   10/21/63

Director, ⟨⟩

SOCIALIST WORKERS PARTY
INTERNAL SECURITY - SWP
DISRUPTION PROGRAM

Reurlet 10/16/63.

Authority is granted for you to prepare and then anonymously mail the letter set out in relet to San Jordan who is running for the office of Mayor of San Francisco as an independent Negro candidate.

The letter should be handwritten on a cheap grade of tablet paper and contain the spelling errors set out in the sample letter enclosed with relet. It should be mailed to him in care of his place of business.

Take the usual precautions to prevent the preparation of the letter and the subsequent mailing of it from being associated with the Bureau. Advise the Bureau when the letter has been mailed and then be alert for any tangible results.

NOTE:

The anonymous letter is ostensibly from a longshoreman who wants to vote for Jordan because of Jordan's strong stand for Negro rights but the writer is concerned because of all the known Social Workers Party (SWP) members who are running Jordan's campaign. The letter indicates, unless Jordan gets rid of the SWP members, many people who don't want to be branded as a "red" will not support Jordan. The writer of the letter indicates therein he knows Asher Harer, a main spokesman for Jordan, and if the writer identified himself, Harer could make things tough for the writer on the waterfront. The letter has definite disruptive potential.

166

UNITED STATES GOVERNMENT

Memorandum

TO : DIRECTOR, FBI (⬛⬛⬛⬛⬛) · DATE: 2/3/70

FROM : SAC, NEW YORK (⬛⬛⬛⬛⬛)

SUBJECT: COINTELPRO - NEW LEFT

Reference is made to New York letter dated 1/14/70.

Enclosed are two copies of a suggested "memorandum" concerning the National Steering Committee of the New Mobilization Committee To End The War In Vietnam (NMC), which is designed to cause splits within NMC leadership by pitting the non-Trotskyites against radicals who are members of the Socialist Workers Party (SWP). It is also designed to bring to the fore the small number of Blacks actually serving on the steering committee.

Bureau authority is requested for New York to prepare enclosed memorandum and mail anonymously to all members of the NMC Steering Committee and other selected officals in the organization. Copies will also be sent to selected officals of the Vietnam Moratorium Committee in Washington, D. C.

Pages 167 and 168: *"To cause splits within NMC," the FBI in 1970 sent a fake letter blaming the SWP for alleged exclusion of Blacks from the antiwar coalition.*

NEW MOBILIZATION COMMITTEE TO END THE WAR IN VIETNAM
1029 Vermont Avenue, N.W., Washington, D.C. 20005
Area Code 212 737-8600

MEMO TO: National Steering Committee

RE: The Absolute Racial Imbalance of the NSC

Having for a short time served as a member of the NSC, and
currently active in the Moratorium Committee - both in
Washington and New York, I find it necessary to call attention
to certain facts overlooked or shovelled under the rug by
NMC leadership.

My understanding at the time I joined NMC was that it was to
be run as a non-exclusionary organization - devoted to one
primary cause, the immediate end of the frightful war in
Vietnam. We were not to be side-tracked into supporting
the aims of the militant left. We were not to be sucked
into protests against the government's trial of the Conspiracy
8 in Chicago and the like. Our sights were to be adjusted
at some later time when the war terminated. Or, so I thought.

Over the past several years the Trotskyites have literally
taken control of the body proper and have repeatedly resisted
efforts to recruit black brothers into NMC leadership. In
addition, they have seen fit to use the good offices of
the NMC to further their own political aspirations, nebulous
as they are.

I have been sickened - on more than one occasion - by the
promises made to the Black United Front, promises not kept,
promises made with the mouth and not the heart. The attitude
of the Steering Committee towards the BUF was and is a
matter of disgrace. In the main, NMC leadership has been
no better than the racist politicians and phony liberals
who give lip service to the black community and turn their
backs on any positive action.

The NMC leadership has demonstrated an appalling lack of
sensitivity towards the largest minority in the country.
If NMC is to survive the coming months, the situation
must be rectified immediately. Our leadership - including
the omni-present Trotskyites and other radicals - had better
take positive steps before those who disagree with current
policy, and there are many, either withhold future support
or take decisive action to remove NMC leadership. It is
my belief the NMC would greatly benefit under a leader like
Sam Brown of MC.

To avoid senseless imbroglio, I choose to remain anonymous
until the proper time. Just for the record - I am not
Black.....

April 4, 1962

Airtel

To: SAC, New York (   )
From: Director, FBI (   )

COMMUNIST PARTY, USA
COUNTERINTELLIGENCE PROGRAM
INTERNAL SECURITY - C

       In the 4/1/62 issue of "The Worker" on page 10, an advertisement appears for a social affair to be held 4/6/62 at the Bitter End Cafe, 147 Bleecker Street, to commemorate one "Paddy Mehir, IRA hero - Union leader." The advertisement states tickets are available at three locations, one of which is listed as "Socialist Workers Party City Office - 116 University Place."

       It has always been a firm policy of the Communist Party (CP) not to consider any cooperation with or assistance to the Socialist Workers Party (SWP) especially in the use of advertising space in the columns of "The Worker." This advertisement in the 4/1/62 issue must have been arranged through some contacts by "The Worker" staff with SWP members. This appears to offer an opportunity to carry out a counterintelligence operation.

       New York should consider making an anonymous telephone call to "The Worker" office accusing the officials of becoming so capitalistic that they are getting financial support by giving advertising space to the SWP. It can also be pointed out that this situation will lead to the paper being infiltrated by the Trotskyites. New York can also consider an anonymous telephone call to SWP officials to make the accusation that some traitor must be doing business with the CP.

       If it appears that a controversial issue is being created over this matter, security informants participating

Pages 169–171: A 1962 anonymous phone call operation to promote hostility between the Socialist Workers party and the Communist party, which were cooperating in defense of the Irish struggle.

Airtel to New York
RE: COMMUNIST PARTY, USA
    COUNTERINTELLIGENCE PROGRAM

in the Counterintelligence Program of your office should
be directed to raise further criticism of the CP's
abandonment of the long-standing principle of no
association with the SWP.

Advise the Bureau of the action taken by
your office. Promptly furnish any tangible results.

NOTE ON YELLOW:

Airtel is being used to enable the New York Office
to handle this matter while "The Worker" issue of 4/1/62
is still current.

170

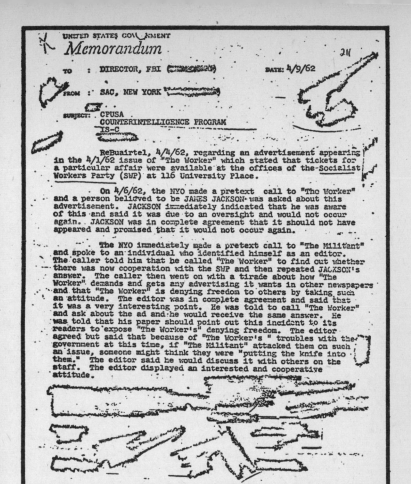

UNITED STATES GOVERNMENT

Memorandum   211

TO   : DIRECTOR, FBI (━━━━━)   DATE: 4/9/62

FROM : SAC, NEW YORK ━━━━━

SUBJECT: CPUSA
          COUNTERINTELLIGENCE PROGRAM
          IS-C

ReBuairtel, 4/4/62, regarding an advertisement appearing
in the 4/1/62 issue of "The Worker" which stated that tickets for
a particular affair were available at the offices of the Socialist
Workers Party (SWP) at 116 University Place.

On 4/6/62, the NYO made a pretext call to "The Worker"
and a person believed to be JAMES JACKSON was asked about this
advertisement. JACKSON immediately indicated that he was aware
of this and said it was due to an oversight and would not occur
again. JACKSON was in complete agreement that it should not have
appeared and promised that it would not occur again.

The NYO immediately made a pretext call to "The Militant"
and spoke to an individual who identified himself as an editor.
The caller told him that he called "The Worker" to find out whether
there was now cooperation with the SWP and then repeated JACKSON's
answer. The caller then went on with a tirade about how "The
Worker" demands and gets any advertising it wants in other newspapers
and that "The Worker" is denying freedom to others by taking such
an attitude. The editor was in complete agreement and said that
it was a very interesting point. He was told to call "The Worker"
and ask about the ad and he would receive the same answer. He
was told that his paper should point out this incident to its
readers to expose "The Worker's" denying freedom. The editor
agreed but said that because of "The Worker's" troubles with the
government at this time, if "The Militant" attacked them on such
an issue, someone might think they were "putting the knife into
them." The editor said he would discuss it with others on the
staff. The editor displayed an interested and cooperative
attitude.

171

8 Firing teachers:
"The children and the country deserve to be protected"

In 1968 the FBI took special pride in what it did to Walter Elliot. Elliot was the scoutmaster of Troop 339 in Orange, New Jersey—until the FBI engineered his removal. The FBI said he posed "a distinct threat to the goal of the scouting movement."
Why? Walter Elliot was married to a socialist.

In the view of the bureau, this necessitated a Cointelpro operation to counteract his "strong influence in shaping the minds of young boys." The agent in charge of the effort called Elliot's removal a "successful application of the disruption program for a worthy cause."

The FBI sanctimoniously claims a special duty to "protect young minds." Protect them, that is, from ideas unpopular with the FBI. Teachers prove an obvious target with their strategic "access" to "fertile young minds," as one memo put it.

The Cointelpro files reprinted here show how this crusade to fire teacher activists dovetailed with the FBI's relentless efforts to harass the antiwar movement and drive the Socialist Workers party out of existence.

The case of Evelyn Sell involves an interstate, interagency conspiracy against a preschool teacher described, even by the FBI, as "an intelligent, excellent teacher who was well qualified in her field."

"The decision not to issue a new contract or consider the subject further for employment after the termination of her current contract is based upon information received from [deleted] the Austin Police Department."

That is how the FBI summoned up its efforts in a March 31, 1970, FBI memorandum captioned "Evelyn Rose Sell, SM-SWP"

(Security Matter—Socialist Workers party). This security
matter was in actuality an FBI vendetta against Sell, a Head
Start teacher in Austin, Texas. The top-secret information referred to is the fact that in 1968 Sell ran for public office in
Michigan as an SWP candidate.

This data was sniffed out by the FBI in Detroit at the request
of the San Antonio office and was confidentially passed on to the
Austin police, who then tipped off the Austin Independent
School District. School officials, with this information in hand,
refused to renew Sell's contract at the end of the 1970 school
year.

Today, M.K. Hage, Jr., president of the Austin School Board,
who served on the board when Evelyn Sell was fired, says that
"the social climate was such that we would fire anyone who was
a socialist."

In an interview, Evelyn Sell gave her side of the story.

Before moving to Austin in the summer of 1969, Sell had taught
in the Head Start program in Detroit for four years. She had
helped organize a special unit of the Detroit Federation of
Teachers encompassing the preschool program, and had been a
delegate to the 1969 Michigan Federation of Teachers convention
in the spring of that year.

Sell's political beliefs were no secret. She joined the SWP in
1948 and had been active in socialist politics since then. She was
nominated by the party several times as a candidate for public
office.

"All my cards were on the table," says Sell. "It was the FBI
and the Austin school district officials who were underhanded
and secretive."

It wasn't until after the school district refused to renew her
contract in 1970 that she became aware of the FBI's keen interest in her. The only indication before that time that the FBI was
keeping tabs on her was an incident shortly after she moved to
Austin.

Her son Eric, then a student at Austin High School and an
activist in the Student Mobilization Committee, was called into
his principal's office. There he was informed that the FBI had
paid the school a visit and had told the principal of his antiwar
activities. The principal warned Eric that he was not to organize
any antiwar activities at school, and then added that they were
aware that his mother was a teacher.

"Eric came home and told me about his 'interrogation,' and I
said, 'Well, the FBI must be in contact with my school,' and I

expected to hear something about it. But they never brought it out into the open."

The fall of 1969 saw massive protests against the war, and Austin was no exception with its large university population. Eleven thousand marched to the state capitol for the October 15 Moratorium. And organizing meetings on the campus would draw from 100 to 150 people. Sell was a consistent participant and organizer of these events.

Did she connect her antiwar activity with the decision not to renew her contract in 1970?

"I suspected at the time that the FBI may have had something to do with it. The school used the excuse that the Head Start program, which had been administered by the school district, was no longer under its control. But I knew that was a phony excuse," Sell recalls.

"Texas had passed a law establishing a kindergarten system for the first time in its history, and they had very few qualified teachers. As a matter of fact, they were scrounging around trying to find teachers who had kindergarten endorsements. I was one of the few who had such an endorsement from the Texas Education Agency. And I asked to be retained by the school district to teach in the new kindergarten program."

When Sell's contract was not renewed, she immediately applied to the local poverty agency that took over direction of the Head Start program, the Human Opportunities Corporation. She was accepted as an educational services supervisor. By early 1971 she had been promoted to director of the Child Development Program.

The FBI files released on Sell end with the notation that Sell had been hired by the HOC and that the information about her socialist activities would be furnished to that agency.

What the files don't report is that the FBI streamed in and out of the HOC offices, repeatedly visiting at least three of Sell's supervisors in an attempt to convince them that, qualified or not, this socialist did not deserve a job. One reason they offered was her active participation in the women's movement. Sell had played a leading role in organizing a demonstration in support of the right to abortion.

"The HOC directors were outraged by the visits," Sell says. "One of them told me that he was seriously considering filing a lawsuit against the FBI because of the harassing visits."

The HOC resisted the FBI pressure because they considered Sell an asset to the program. In her personal files, Sell has a letter from the parents' council of Head Start praising her for her work. It says in part:

"We wish to commend Mrs. Evelyn Sell . . . for a job *well* done! Her fairness and efficiency and her willingness to always make herself readily available if she could be of any help in any situation was quickly recognized." (The emphasis is in the original.)

Sell left the Head Start program in January 1972, not because the FBI visits frightened or intimidated her, but because she was again to run for public office as a socialist in the 1972 elections.

"But I don't doubt that the FBI visits continued until the day I left," Sell comments. "And they certainly continued past the April 1971 'termination' of the FBI Cointelpros."

The Starsky Case

Prominent in the ranks of teachers victimized by the FBI is Morris Starsky. In 1970 the FBI encouraged Starsky's dismissal from his job as a professor of philosophy at Arizona State University. The Phoenix office of the FBI sent an anonymous letter slandering him to a faculty committee reviewing his teaching contract.

In a memo dated May 31, 1968, the Phoenix FBI noted that local targets for Cointelpro were "pretty obvious. . . . It is apparent that New Left organizations and activities in the Phoenix metropolitan area have received their inspiration and leadership almost exclusively from the members of the faculty in the Department of Philosophy at Arizona State University (ASU), chiefly Assistant Professor MORRIS J. STARSKY."

To that description of himself, Starsky adds that he helped organize the first antiwar teach-in at ASU; he led a campus free speech fight; he helped lead a successful campaign to win campus recognition for SDS; he participated in campus activities to support striking Tucson sanitation workers and a union organizing drive by Chicago laundry workers; he served as a presidential elector for the Socialist Workers party in 1968; he helped to reestablish the ASU chapter of the American Federation of Teachers; and he was the faculty adviser of the Young Socialist Alliance and the Student Mobilization Committee.

All that provoked quite a furor among right-wing state legislators and university regents. The Faculty Committee on Academic Freedom and Tenure (whose members received the FBI's slanderous letters) held a hundred hours of public hearings on whether Starsky was entitled to teach at ASU. Three thousand students and over 250 professors signed petitions supporting Starsky's right to academic freedom.

The committee's members were not duped by the FBI's anonymous slanders, although they expressed surprise five years later when they learned that "A Concerned Alumnus" was really J. Edgar Hoover. The committee voted unanimously against dismissing Starsky. But the regents refused to renew his contract and he lost his job in June 1970. Starsky says that "it's sort of like being found innocent and executed anyway." Since ASU he has lost two teaching jobs in California for political reasons.

Starsky calls the FBI drive against him an attack on the rights of everyone. "What teacher is safe?" he asks. "What ideas would not subject a teacher to this kind of attack?—only U.S. government approved ideas."

Starsky has spent the past five years fighting for his rights in and out of court. He has won one damage suit already. And an Arizona court ruled that the ASU action violated his civil rights. Meanwhile, the FBI refuses to turn over to Starsky some of its files on him on the grounds of "national security."

"I've taught a couple of logic courses," he says, "but I had a hard time figuring out how my seeing my own files would harm national security. After I read the Cointelpro documents it became clear: 'national security' means the FBI's security from the nation finding out the vicious things it does in violation of people's civil liberties."

More Poison Pen Letters

FBI schemes to get two other teachers fired are documented here. Unlike the Sell and Starsky cases, these efforts did not have the results the FBI wanted.

In 1969 the Detroit office received approval from Washington to send a series of letters on Professor David Herreshoff to Michigan State Senator Robert Huber. Huber was chairman of a legislative committee investigating student dissent on state campuses.

The letters were signed "A Fed-up Taxpayer!" They document seventeen years of Herreshoff's political activity from 1951, when he was a student at the University of Minnesota, through 1968, while he was a member of the faculty at Wayne State University.

Compiled from "public source material" to ensure the FBI could not be identified as the letters' source, the information was intended to make a case for ridding Wayne State of Herreshoff's "peculiar" influence.

Herreshoff's "disruptive" activities apparently included a debate with a former FBI agent in 1951 on the topic "Does the FBI Menace Civil Liberties?"; his participation in the University of Minnesota's Socialist Club, which spearheaded a campaign in 1955 to remove campus restrictions on outside speakers; and his election to the Detroit executive board of the American Civil Liberties Union. Herreshoff says he is "happy that everything charged against me in the FBI 'denunciation' is true."

Herreshoff recalls that during the debate with the FBI agent he accused the agency of "breaking the law every day in the week. That was back in 1951. I guess the FBI never forgets an insult."

Herreshoff says he doesn't believe the FBI will ever change and it ought to be abolished. "Wouldn't abolishing the FBI be a fitting observation of the bicentennial of the revolution?"

In still another poison pen episode, the FBI tried in April 1969 to get Maude White (now Wilkinson) "separated from her employment" as a preschool teacher in Washington, D.C. The local FBI sent an anonymous letter signed "A Concerned Citizen," purporting to be from Wilkinson's neighbor, to the superintendent of the D.C. school system. The letter said that "Miss White has held weekly meetings of a socialist youth group" in her apartment.

After expounding upon the classical FBI distortions of the YSA as a group supporting "violent activities against established authority," the letter continues, "I bring this information to your attention in order to protect the D.C. School System from the menace of a teacher who does not have the interests of the children or the country at heart."

But it was precisely the interests of the children and the American people that led Wilkinson to become a socialist: "Being a teacher, especially in the D.C. schools, I saw how rotten the schools were, how much money was spent on war and how little on education," she says.

Wilkinson's files also document the three-way collusion between the FBI, the intelligence unit of the Washington police, and the school administration. According to an FBI memo, one local cop was delegated responsibility for conducting intelligence investigations within the D.C. school system at the direction of the assistant superintendent of schools in charge of personnel.

Information on Wilkinson compiled by the D.C. police was forwarded to the FBI.

The Response From Teachers

The revelation of such attacks on teachers has evoked an outraged response from educators and civil libertarians alike. Professor William Van Alstyne, president of the American Association of University Professors, demanded that the agents responsible for the "sleazy and surreptitious campaigns" against Morris Starsky be fired. Delegates to the 1975 national convention of the AAUP gave the former professor a warm welcome and voted to support his efforts to defend academic freedom. Local chapters of the AAUP and the American Federation of Teachers cosponsored many of Starsky's speaking engagements during a nationwide tour he conducted in the spring of 1975 to win support for the SWP suit.

Publications with large circulations among educators, including *Higher Education Daily*, *Chronicle of Higher Education*, the AAUP's *Academe*, and the AFT's *American Teacher*, printed articles criticizing the Cointelpro attacks.

At the 1975 national convention of the 1.7 million member National Education Association, Executive Secretary Terry Herndon condemned the FBI's operations as "reminiscent of the witch-hunts during the McCarthy era," noting that nowhere does the FBI charge that any one of its targets was not a good teacher.

Herndon asked a question that must be on many people's minds: "While only a few such cases have surfaced thus far, we cannot help wondering how many more teachers were dismissed or harassed because of counterproductive surreptitious activity by the FBI into the private lives of educators." The NEA leader added, "Such efforts to get teachers fired only make the job of teaching about democracy and government that much harder."

The head of Maude Wilkinson's chapter of the NEA summoned it up well. In a telephone interview, John Radcliffe told of his immediate response to the Cointelpro operations.

"As soon as I found out about the situation," Radcliffe said, "I called the school district and told them that . . . we, acting as the union, would absolutely and categorically not tolerate anyone messing with Maude's job."

Radcliffe has no doubt that the FBI is continuing its efforts to get people with dissident views fired. But he thinks that the political climate has changed and that the FBI doesn't have such an easy time of it today. "As far as Maude's job goes in Fairfax County, it's secure," Radcliffe concluded. "She can belong to any political party she wants to."

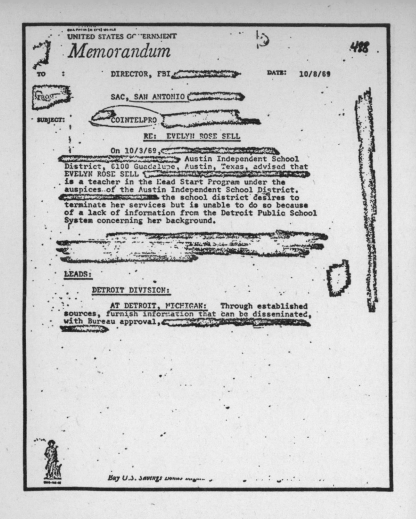

UNITED STATES GOVERNMENT

Memorandum

488

TO : DIRECTOR, FBI ~~████~~ DATE: 10/8/69

FROM : SAC, SAN ANTONIO ~~████~~

SUBJECT: COINTELPRO ~~████~~

RE: EVELYN ROSE SELL

On 10/3/69, ~~████~~ Austin Independent School District, 6100 Guadelupe, Austin, Texas, advised that EVELYN ROSE SELL ~~████~~ is a teacher in the Head Start Program under the auspices of the Austin Independent School District. ~~████~~ the school district desires to terminate her services but is unable to do so because of a lack of information from the Detroit Public School System concerning her background.

LEADS:

DETROIT DIVISION:

AT DETROIT, MICHIGAN: Through established sources, furnish information that can be disseminated, with Bureau approval, ~~████~~

Buy U.S. Savings Bonds ~~████~~

Initial FBI memo suggesting the Detroit office seek out information on Evelyn Sell that could be furnished to the Austin, Texas, school board.

180

The Head Start Program will be operated by an independent group commencing with the 1970-1971 school year and will no longer be under the auspices of the Austin Independent School District.

The subject was described as an' intelligent, excellent teacher who was well qualified in her field.

Bureau attention is directed to San Antonio letter to the Bureau captioned "COINTELPRO, IS - DISRUPTION OF NEW LEFT," ~~~~~~~~~~~~~~~~~~~~~~ dated 1/13/70. ~~~~~~~~~~~~~~~~ the decision not to issue a new contract or consider the subject further for employment after the termination of her current contract is based upon information received from ~~~~~~~~~~~~~~~~~~~~~~ the Austin Police Department. ~~~~~~~~~~~~~~~~~~~~~~~ information furnished ~~~~~~~~~~~~~ would be furnished to the organization which will be handling the Head Start Program in the 1970-1971 school year.

The third page of a March 31, 1970, memo reporting the success of the bureau's campaign to drive Sell out of her teaching job.

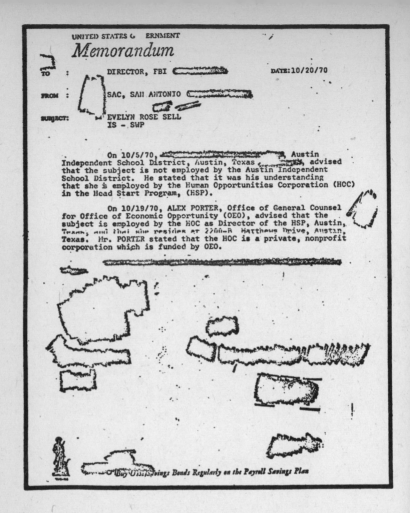

UNITED STATES GOVERNMENT

Memorandum

TO : DIRECTOR, FBI   DATE:10/20/70

FROM : SAC, SAN ANTONIO

SUBJECT: EVELYN ROSE SELL
IS - SWP

On 10/5/70, _____, Austin
Independent School District, Austin, Texas _____, advised
that the subject is not employed by the Austin Independent
School District. He stated that it was his understanding
that she is employed by the Human Opportunities Corporation (HOC)
in the Head Start Program, (HSP).

On 10/19/70, ALEX PORTER, Office of General Counsel
for Office of Economic Opportunity (OEO), advised that the
subject is employed by the HOC as Director of the HSP, Austin,
Texas, and that she resides at 2700-B Matthews Drive, Austin,
Texas. Mr. PORTER stated that the HOC is a private, nonprofit
corporation which is funded by OEO.

Buy U.S. Savings Bonds Regularly on the Payroll Savings Plan

This memo, tracing Sell to her new Head Start job, lays the
groundwork for continued harassment.

182

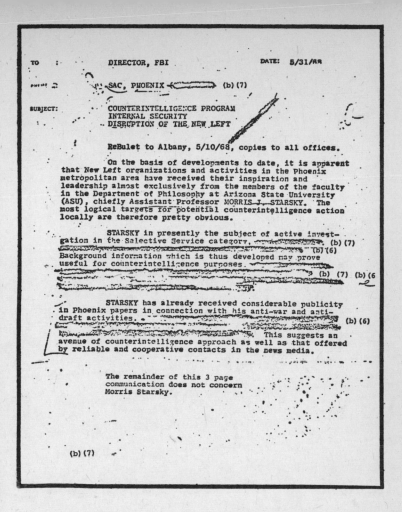

ReBulet to Albany, 5/10/68, copies to all offices.

On the basis of developments to date, it is apparent that New Left organizations and activities in the Phoenix metropolitan area have received their inspiration and leadership almost exclusively from the members of the faculty in the Department of Philosophy at Arizona State University (ASU), chiefly Assistant Professor MORRIS J. STARSKY. The most logical targets for potential counterintelligence action locally are therefore pretty obvious.

STARSKY in presently the subject of active investigation in the Selective Service category. ~~~~~~~~~~~ (b) (7)
~~~~~~ (b) (6)
Background information which is thus developed may prove useful for counterintelligence purposes. ~~~~~~~~~~~
~~~~~~ (b) (7) (b) (6)
~~~~~~~~~~~~~~~~~~~~~~~~~~~~~~~

STARSKY has already received considerable publicity in Phoenix papers in connection with his anti-war and anti-draft activities. ~~~~~~~~~~~~~~~~~~~~~~~~~ (b) (6)
~~~~~~~~~~~~~~~~~~~~~~~~~~~~~~~~~~~~~ This suggests an avenue of counterintelligence approach as well as that offered by reliable and cooperative contacts in the news media.

The remainder of this 3 page communication does not concern Morris Starsky.

(b) (7)

Pages 183 and 184: Letters from the Phoenix office targeting Professor Morris Starsky, described as an antiwar activist and SWP presidential elector, for disruption.

Memorandum

TO : DIRECTOR, FBI (⸺) (b) (7)   DATE: 10/1/68

FROM : SAC, PHOENIX (⸺) (b) (7)

SUBJECT: COUNTERINTELLIGENCE PROGRAM
INTERNAL SECURITY
DISRUPTION OF THE NEW LEFT

Remylet, 7/1/68.

1. Potential Counterintelligence Action

MORRIS J. STARSKY, by his actions, has continued to spotlight himself as a target for counterintelligence action. He and his wife were both named as presidential electors by and for the Socialist Workers Party when the SWP in August, 1968, gained a place on the ballot in Arizona. In addition they have signed themselves as treasurer and secretary respectively of the Arizona SWP. Professor STARSKY's status at Arizona State University may be affected by the outcome of his pending trial on charges of disturbing the peace. He is alleged to have used violent, abusive and obscene language against the Assistant Managing Director of Gammage Auditorium at ASU during memorial services for MARTIN LUTHER KING last April. Trial is now scheduled for 10/8/68 in Justice Court, Tempe, Arizona.

A recommendation for counterintelligence action as to STARSKY will be submitted by separate letter.

The remainder of this 2 page communication does not concern Morris Starsky.

(b) (7)

Bureau approval is requested to mail a copy of the enclosed anonymous letter to each member of the faculty committee which is hearing the charges against STARSKY. This committee is sitting in the Law School on the ASU campus and is composed of the following faculty members:

1. Dr. ROSS R. RICE, Chairman.

2. JOHN A. COCHRAN

3. RICHARD W. EFFLAND

4. JOHN P. DECKER

5. WALLACE ADAMS, Chairman of the Faculty Assembly.

Pages 185 and 186: The Phoenix FBI sought and received permission to send members of a faculty committee an anonymous letter slandering Starsky.

Dear Sir:

It seems appropriate that you should be informed
of one of the most recent activities of Morris J. Starsky.
Starsky learned of a suicide attempt by one of his close campus
co-workers, David Murphy. Feeling that Murphy could no longer
be trusted as a member of the campus socialist group, Starsky
demanded that Murphy return all literature and other materials
belonging to the socialist group. Murphy refused to give Starsky
a quantity of socialist literature in his possession until Starsky
would pay him a sum slightly in excess of $50 which was owed for
telephone calls charged by Starsky to Murphy's telephone. Morris
Starsky was indignant at Murphy's independent attitude and at
2:00 A. M. on April 5, 1970 he, accompanied by his wife Pamela
and two young male associates, invaded Murphy's apartment and
under threat demanded return of the socialist literature. When
Murphy refused unless Starsky paid the phone bill, Starsky told
him that his two associates would beat him unmercifully. Murphy,
convalescing from a recent hospital stay, was under great fear
of bodily harm or death and surrendered the literature.

I find this episode interesting. Where did Starsky
learn of the effectiveness of smashing into a person's home at
2:00 A. M.? Also, of utilizing four persons to threaten the
health or life of someone? Is this an example of academic
socialism? Should the ASU student body enjoy the guidance of
such an instructor? It seems to me that this type of activity
is something that Himmler or Beria could accept with pride. If
Starsky did not enjoy the prestige and sanctuary of his position
he would be properly punished for such a totalitarian venture.
Unfortunately, Murphy is too terrified to testify against Starsky.
This is another example of Starsky's brand of academic socialism.

/s/ A concerned ASU alumnus

186

ROUTE IN ENVELOPE

*Leaving little to chance, FBI headquarters directed Phoenix
to "delete caption 'Anonymous Letter . . .'" before mailing.*

I am indeed pleased to note that you are chairing
a committee to investigate the activities of dissident elements
on our college campuses. I trust that this effort will not
become just another "study" but will actually result in concrete
results to rid our universities and colleges of the disruptive
activities of radicals, leftists and nihilists.

In this connection, I have taken upon myself a small
project regarding the background of Professor David Herreshoff,
of the English Department at Wayne State University.

It occurs to me that our college youth, who are
going through a period of their lives during which they are
most liberal and idealistic in their attitudes, are being
exploited and subverted by certain faculty members in our
colleges. Students by and large, experience these libertarian
attitudes, graduate, then pass into the society and address
themselves to their personal needs and objectives within the
framework of our ongoing society. Very few of them become,
and fewer yet, remain active in radical or disruptive activities
such as campus take overs. However, it is these peculiar
members of faculty who year in and year out use their positions
to imbue the students with the philosophies and ideologies that
provide a continuous stream of chaotic, militant incidents
across the nation.

Why must the taxpayers of this state continually
funnel their money into institutions which provide financial
security and a ready made captive audience to professors who
openly support through word and deed, avowed enemies of this
country? Their heroes are the Che Guevaras, Maoists, Trotskyites,
Stalinists and the anti-Christs. If they support any form of
government at all it is at best socialistic or communistic.

Let these destroyers spew forth their ideas in public
halls to those audiences who seek their words, but let us
deny them speakers platforms in the classrooms of our educational
institutions!

Prof. Herreshoff is active in political action and
social groups existing on the campus at Wayne State University.
However, it is rather enlightening to note which groups these
are. He is the listed faculty sponsor for: the W.E.B. DuBois
Club; Students for a Democratic Society; Student Mobilization
Committee; and, the Young Socialist Alliance. I'm sure you
recognize these "groups" as the very ones continually noted

ENCLOSURE

*Pages 188 and 189: Beginning and end of an eight-page
phony letter supplying FBI-compiled information on Pro-*

.cooperation with the Selective Service System. A protest march took place next to State Hall while the SDS group met with vice-president James Mc Cormick. Prof. David Herreshoff, English instructor, pointed out that the American Civil Liberties Union is preparing to test the constitutionality of various aspects of the draft, including the ranking of students. "The University has taken the position of cooperating with all public bodies", said Herreshoff. "Our group pointed out that some public bodies shouldn't be cooperated with."

An article by David Herreshoff appeared in the May 6, 1968, issue of "The South End", Wayne State University student publication, captioned, "the radical vs. liberal: a view of social order".

An article appearing in the "Detroit News", October 21, 1967, Final edition, captioned "Detroiters Join D.C. Protesters" revealed that while Detroiters waited to board buses outside MacKenzie Hallon the WSU campus for the trip to Washington, D.C., to join the anti-war protesters in a march on the Pentagon, a short rally was held on the steps of State Hall, across Cass Avenue from MacKenzie Hall. Article continues that several speakers, including Dr. David Herreshoff, a Wayne English professor, denounced the United States war effort in Vietnam. Dr. Herreshoff, a frequent campus critic of United States policies, said, "This is not just an American movement—we are part of a world movement". He referred to the "genocidal burning of the people of Vietnam by the people running our country".

On April 24, 1968, an open letter to the student body was published in "The South End", which reads: "We, the undersigned organizations and individuals, urge all students who are against the war in Vietnam to vote on Tuesday and Wednesday in the 'Choice '68' elections for (1) an immediate withdrawal of American forces from Vietnam and (2) a permanent cessation of the bombing of North Vietnam." Among the signatures appeared Dr. David Herreshoff, English Department..

I am preparing more information of this type concerning Prof. Herreshoff and shall send it to you at a later date.

Very truly yours,

A Fed-up Taxpayer!

fessor David Herreshoff to encourage a witch-hunt by a state senator investigating student dissent.

:lliam R. Hanning
Superintendent
D.C. School System
415 12th Street, N.W.
Washington, D.C.

Dear Sir,

I am writing this letter directly to you as Superintendent
of the D.C. School System because of the severity of the accusations
which I am making against a teacher in the D.C. system. I am well
aware of your interest in the quality of education in this, the
Capitol city, and I am sure that you will take a responsible attitude
toward the information which I am furnishing.

As a resident of a large apartment building at 1801 16th
Street, N.W., I have become aware of the activities of another
resident. Miss Maude White, who is a teacher in the local elementary
school at 13th and S Streets, N.W. I have learned that since January
of this year, Miss White has held weekly meetings of a socialist youth
group which is active in the Washington area. From literature found
in our hallways, I have determined that this group is known as the
Young Socialist Alliance and from personal observation I have learned
that approximately twenty individuals attend these meetings each
Sunday evening at Miss White's apartment.

The literature belonging to this group advocates an overthrow
of our present system of government in a way similar to the Cuban
revolution of Fidel Castro. The printed policy of the group supports
violent activities against established authority, particularly the
police, and considers ghetto and student rioting as the beginning of
the violent revolution.

In a recent copy of their national magazine, The Young
Socialist, it is suggested that anyone interested in the organization
can contact Terrill Drumback at 1801 16th Street, N.W., Apartment 610.
This is apparently the same individual who has been living with Miss
White for the last five months. I have noticed him on numerous
occasions parking Diamond Cab #230 in front of the apartment building.

*Pages 190 and 191: This anonymous FBI letter red-baiting
Maude White (Wilkinson) professed to be from "a con-*

190

I bring this information to your attention in order to
.otect the D.C. School System from the menace of a teacher who
.es not have the interests of the children or the country at heart.
I am certain that a responsible school administrator like yourself
could not allow a revolutionist to indoctrinate the fertile minds
of grade school children.

Since most of this information is actually public knowledge, only limited investigation by your office will be necessary
to verify these accusations. For my own protection, I am not signing
this letter. I assure you that this lack of identification in no
way affects the veracity of the information contained herein.

I sincerely hope that your investigation and appropriate
action can be completed before the start of the next semester. I
am sure you will agree that the children and the country deserve to
be protected.

A Concerned Citizen

cerned citizen" worried that she would "indoctrinate the
fertile minds of grade school children."

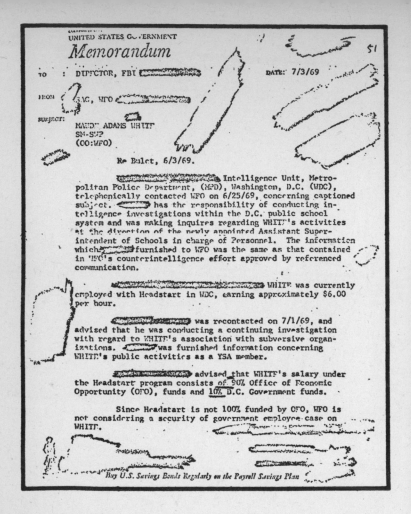

UNITED STATES GOVERNMENT

Memorandum   51

TO   : DIRECTOR, FBI ▓▓▓▓▓▓▓▓▓   DATE: 7/3/69

FROM   : (SAC, WFO ▓▓▓▓▓▓▓▓▓

SUBJECT:
         MAUDE ADAMS WHITE
         SM-SWP
         (OO:WFO)

                 Re Bulet, 6/3/69.

                 ▓▓▓▓▓▓▓▓▓▓▓ Intelligence Unit, Metro-
         politan Police Department, (MPD), Washington, D.C. (WDC),
         telephonically contacted WFO on 6/25/69, concerning captioned
         subject. ▓▓▓▓▓ has the responsibility of conducting in-
         telligence investigations within the D.C. public school
         system and was making inquires regarding WHITE's activities
         at the direction of the newly appointed Assistant Super-
         intendent of Schools in charge of Personnel. The information
         which ▓▓▓▓▓ furnished to WFO was the same as that contained
         in WFO's counterintelligence effort approved by referenced
         communication.

                 ▓▓▓▓▓▓▓▓▓▓▓▓▓▓▓ WHITE was currently
         employed with Headstart in WDC, earning approximately $6.00
         per hour.

                 ▓▓▓▓▓▓▓▓▓ was recontacted on 7/1/69, and
         advised that he was conducting a continuing investigation
         with regard to WHITE's association with subversive organ-
         izations. ▓▓▓▓▓ was furnished information concerning
         WHITE's public activities as a YSA member.

                 ▓▓▓▓▓▓▓▓▓ advised that WHITE's salary under
         the Headstart program consists of 90% Office of Economic
         Opportunity (OEO), funds and 10% D.C. Government funds.

                 Since Headstart is not 100% funded by OEO, WFO is
         not considering a security of government employee case on
         WHITE.

         Buy U.S. Savings Bonds Regularly on the Payroll Savings Plan

*This 1969 FBI memo documents the systematic collabora-
tion of the bureau, school administrators, and the local
police red squad to hunt down and purge leftist teachers.*

9 The fight to stop Cointelpro goes before the public

Peter Camejo and Syd Stapleton walked into NBC's Washington studios at 6:15 on the morning of March 19, 1975. At 7:00 a.m. the "Today" show went on the air. A few minutes later millions of Americans first learned of the FBI's conspiracy to destroy the Socialist Workers party.

Readers of the *New York Times* who had picked up that day's paper when it hit the street the night before were the first to find out about the story. The main headline was about the CIA's multi-million-dollar operation to retrieve a Soviet submarine off the floor of the Pacific. But also on the front page was an account of the FBI's Cointelpro plot against the socialists.

Peter Camejo is the SWP's presidential candidate. Syd Stapleton is national secretary of the Political Rights Defense Fund. After their appearance on the "Today" program, they drove to a news conference. There the PRDF released copies of the Cointelpro papers and individual FBI files on several SWP members.

Soon after the Washington news conference, reporters dispatched stories about the contents of the FBI files to newspapers and television and radio stations across the country. That evening and the next morning millions more learned about the FBI plot against their democratic rights.

In the following weeks the PRDF amassed some 600 newspaper clippings on this story. While this hardly compared to the deluge of publicity surrounding the Watergate scandal, it did represent an important breakthrough in alerting the American people to the systematic crimes of the federal spy agencies. The coverage in the major news media, reaching tens of millions of people, included the following:

• A March 19 Associated Press dispatch was carried in 1970 daily papers in thirty-seven states. It was front-page news in 50 papers.

• The *New York Times* ran a detailed page-one story, plus a background article on the SWP. The *Times* story was picked up by at least twenty-five dailies.

• The AP sent out five separate follow-up articles.

• United Press International distributed two different stories.

• The *Washington Post* carried a page-one article.

• It's more difficult to measure the response on radio and television, although most Americans rely on them for news. The "Today" interview was the most significant.

"The major papers all carried at least one story on the documents," said Cathy Perkus of the PRDF national staff. "The press treated the story very seriously. They saw the FBI behavior revealed in the documents as illegal and unjustifiable. I believe they accepted our assertion that these sorts of things are still going on." The charge that Cointelpro continues—whatever it's now called—is central to the suit.

The front page of the March 20 *Houston Chronicle* carried a big headline about Dan Fein's FBI file. He had been the SWP's candidate for mayor in the previous election.

Newspapers in Minnesota, New Jersey, New York, and Wisconsin ran stories about illegal FBI activity in their areas.

The *Los Angeles Times* sent a staff writer to Arizona to report on what happened to Morris Starsky, the Cointelpro victim who was fired from his teaching position at Arizona State University. The reporter called FBI headquarters in Washington to ask why the FBI had launched this attack on Starsky and the SWP. The FBI refused to comment. But, interestingly, they did send him a copy of red-baiting remarks inserted into the *Congressional Record* by Representative Larry McDonald, a leading member of the John Birch Society.

A good many of the files involved attacks on the Black civil rights movement. Several North Carolina papers printed stories on an operation in that state. One of the AP stories, which concerned the North Carolina incident, was featured in papers throughout the South.

New York City's major Black paper, the *Amsterdam News*, ran a front-page story on FBI attempts to block collaboration between the NAACP and socialists. Syndicated Black political commentator Chuck Stone wrote about how the new interest in

Marxism among some Blacks relates to the FBI assault on the SWP.

The *Guild Reporter*, put out by the Newspaper Guild, described how the "FBI misused the press."

The *Militant* has provided the most thorough coverage by far of the Cointelpro story—with several news articles and a twelve-part "Cointelpro Papers" series.

Others reporting the story included important papers in several different countries, campus papers, Liberation News Service, *Rights* magazine, and "alternative newspapers" in many cities.

Three months later, on June 24, the PRDF turned over to the news media a new group of files coughed up by the FBI. Again, it was big news.

The major national news sources—AP, UPI, the *New York Times*, the *Washington Post*—all featured stories. Syd Stapleton appeared on the network "CBS Morning News."

The release of the documents rated banner headlines in the *Houston Chronicle*, the *Cleveland Plain Dealer*, and the *Washington Star*—all papers in cities where FBI dirty work was uncovered.

Stories on other local Cointelpro plots unmasked by the files were featured in newspapers in St. Louis; Milwaukee; Atlanta; Detroit, Kalamazoo, and Muskegon, Michigan; Indianapolis; Portland; and Austin. Some of these stories were in turn reprinted in other cities.

Muhammad Speaks (now *Bilalian News*) covered an Atlanta PRDF news conference where it was revealed that the FBI worked with the *Atlanta Constitution* to red-bait the YSA and the antiwar movement in that city in 1968. (The *Constitution* was the only paper to suggest the FBI files might be forgeries.)

Perhaps more revealing than the level of news coverage was the amount and character of editorial comment. The PRDF has received editorials on the first set of files alone from thirty-six newspapers.

Several columnists commented in one way or another on the release of the Cointelpro papers. Included were nationally syndicated columnists Nicholas Von Hoffman, Mary McGrory, Tom Wicker, Arthur Hoppe, and Patrick Owens. James Wechsler, an editor of the *New York Post*, devoted two of his daily columns to the subject, and *Village Voice* columnist Nat Hentoff mentioned it.

Conservative political commentator James J. Kilpatrick criticized the FBI's actions in remarks broadcast nationwide on the CBS radio network.

Taken together this media response presents an illuminating picture of the current controversy around the role of the FBI.

The first thing that stands out is that nowhere is there any attempt at all to defend the Cointelpro conspiracy. On the contrary, it comes in for scathing criticism: "To the list of organized crime operations, add the FBI. . . . thoroughly illegal"—*Dayton* (Ohio) *Daily News.* "Tactics ranging from the bizarre to the despicable"—*Des Moines* (Iowa) *Register.* "Frightening, chilling"—*Philadelphia Inquirer.* "Illegal and unconstitutional"—*Niagara Falls* (New York) *Gazette.* "Gutter tactics"— Ogdensburg (New York) *Advance-News.* "Gestapo tactics"—*St. Louis Post-Dispatch.* "It reads a lot like lies and libel . . . like a mixture of the late Joseph McCarthy and the worst of Watergate."—Bruce Morton, "CBS Morning News."

Kilpatrick's remarks over CBS radio must have articulated the feelings of many who share his political views: "I hope to remain a friend of the bureau, but the disclosure of the FBI's outrageous and contemptible harassment of the Social Workers party is enough to put a crimp in any friendship."

Many observers have noted the SWP's legality: "A legal American political party. . . . not accused of violating any laws"—*St. Louis Pioneer Press.* "Views never were shown to be subversive or in any way endangering freedom in our democracy"—*Blade,* Toledo, Ohio. "Perfectly lawful American political party, entitled to exist alongside the Republican party [and] the Democratic party"—Charleston, West Virginia, *Gazette-Mail.* "Legal political party"—*Minneapolis Star.*

Conspicuously absent for the most part is any tone of old-fashioned red-baiting. As the Scranton, Pennsylvania *Times* saw it, their "sin in the eyes of J. Edgar Hoover [was] believing that a brand of socialism would be better economically and politically for the United States than the present system."

After making points like those, many observers went out of their way to insert some disparaging remark about the SWP. A couple of editorials described the SWP as insignificant.

On the one hand, these writers think the FBI is urgently in need of a face-lifting to recapture its authority, and this is their way of putting the FBI down for what they see as wasting time and money.

But it isn't very surprising that the SWP is described in this way. The party is small by most standards. Certainly, in terms of American political parties—where the capitalist Democratic and Republican parties monopolize the scene—the SWP seems irrelevant to most commentators. Some were no doubt genuinely confused about why the FBI paid so much attention to the SWP and YSA. It was a sign of J. Edgar Hoover's "paranoia," concluded a few.

J. Edgar Hoover, in any case, is not central to the issue. There is ample evidence that Cointelpro-type operations continue after his death. But for all his idiosyncracies, he was a devoted servant of the ruling class. His job was to run a political police force—one that was cloaked in secrecy—and he did just that for fifty years. It is dirty work.

Most people believe that in a democracy there is not really supposed to be a secret police. Cointelpro, as a matter of fact, was never meant to be known to the American people. That's why Hoover made a big display of canceling the program after it came to light in 1971.

The Cointelpro papers and the other files reveal some stupid FBI blunders and misestimates. The total picture, however, is of cool, calculating technicians, not crazed paranoids, going about the business of secretly combating people who are challenging the rule of the rich. That's the FBI's job.

The American ruling class is very farsighted. Although socialism is still relatively uninfluential in the political life of this country, that is not true on a world scale. The rulers realize this. They foresee a potential socialist challenge here. They study the history of past American radicalizations in which socialists have been prominent. They can also see—more clearly than many media commentators—that socialists have had some role in current social struggles.

In an interview with *Newsday*, Peter Camejo put it this way: "Hoover realized you can't judge a movement only by numbers. He realized that the party was a catalyst in the anti war movement. Break us and you've broken the back of the anti-war movement, is the way he reasoned it."

All the big newspapers and television and radio networks are owned by wealthy capitalists. They have an interest in how the dispute over the FBI and CIA is finally resolved. Commentary in the news media is a reflection of a discussion now going on in ruling circles.

There is wide agreement that both the FBI and CIA need a new coat of paint. That was the goal of the Congressional and

Enough Is Enough

The official position of the Federal Bureau of Investigation and the Department of Justice on the bureau's counterintelligence program (Cointelpro) is that it was foolish, misguided and sometimes illegal and that it was ended in April, 1971. Yet, according to F.B.I. documents recently obtained by the Socialist Workers' party in a lawsuit against the bureau, some Cointelpro techniques were being employed at least as late as December, 1973.

The documents show that after April, 1971, the bureau continued to contact members of the Socialist Workers' party and its youth affiliate to inform them of the bureau's knowledge of their political activities and then to seek more information about those activities. The bureau also continued to contact members of the organization by telephone to gain personal information about them under the pretext of doing a jury duty survey. Such methods were used on at least 34 occasions after the program was supposedly ended.

The Socialist Workers' party is a legal American political organization. Although it has been the subject of wiretap surveillance for thirty years, no indictments and no convictions have been obtained by the Government. The only conceivable purpose of the continuation of the Cointelpro techniques is harassment and disruption of legitimate political activity.

Attorney General Levi has recently expressed his high regard for the F.B.I. and has characterized some recent criticism of the organization as unfounded. The criticism might fade more quickly if it were clear to the bureau that disruption of legitimate political activity is not part of its mandate and if it could be demonstrated to the American people that when the Government says it has terminated a course of improper conduct, it actually has done so.

other government-sponsored investigations. The *New York Times* has urged "the slumbering F.B.I. oversight committees in Congress . . . to develop some clear new rules of conduct for the bureau."

Writing in the *Saturday Review*, former CIA official Tom Braden predicted, "Various committees now investigating the agency will doubtless find error. They will recommend change; they will reshuffle. But they will leave the monster intact."

But even though some intended the investigations to be merely cosmetic, they have played an important part in focusing public attention on the abuses of the intelligence agencies. They have sometimes led to uncovering *new* scandals that compounded the problem of restoring credibility to the institutions. That's what happened with the discoveries of CIA assassinations and FBI burglaries.

New FBI Director Clarence Kelley has taken steps to improve the agency's image. He has given frequent news conferences and interviews, something Hoover shied away from. Local FBI offices, which have always refused to talk to the media, have been sending agents for special training in public relations.

The socialist suit raises more substantial questions than the FBI's image. It calls for a halt not only to Cointelpro-style harassment but to political surveillance. A short-lived victory was won in December 1974 when a federal judge banned FBI spying at the YSA's annual convention. The temporary ruling was later substantially weakened by Supreme Court Justice Thurgood Marshall.

"No responsible Government official now advocates a total ban on electronic surveillance," the *New York Time*'s Nicholas Horrock wrote. That remains true.

None of the editorials came out and squarely condemned spying. A couple of papers explicitly endorsed it. The problem was that the FBI "went beyond keeping an eye on the group"— *Atlanta Journal*.

In an article on the Congressional investigations into the FBI, Horrock found that "the F.B.I. has been far less criticized for investigations leading to prosecutions than it was for its so-called 'counterintelligence program.' "

Attorney General Edward Levi has offered a rather half-hearted criticism of Cointelpro. He labeled the operation "foolish because [it] doesn't work very well" and "outrageous because I think there's enough dishonesty and lack of candor and incivility in our society as it is."

FBI Director Kelley hasn't even gone that far. In fact, he has openly defended Cointelpro. It was meant "to do something that would ultimately . . . benefit the nation," he said.

A retired FBI official, former assistant director William A. Sullivan, was even more forthright in his endorsement of the conspiracy. On July 6, 1975, he appeared—with Kelley's blessings—on CBS-TV's "Face the Nation." A reporter asked about the SWP Cointelpro. Sullivan endorsed sending letters to employers to get SWP members fired. "The only mistake that I think that we make in an instance like that was sending an anonymous letter and not signing J. Edgar Hoover's name to it. I think we owe the American people this type of information."

In an earlier interview with the campus newspaper of the University of California at Los Angeles, Sullivan was asked if there is "any law that allows the FBI to expose Communists." He said he knew of none. But, he added, "there is not any that I know of that say that we should not do this either."

During the "Face the Nation" interview Sullivan was forced to admit that the SWP had done nothing illegal. "We have no evidence to this date that I know of that they've ever been involved in any violent activities," he said.

Then why is the FBI so interested in the SWP? Sullivan told the UCLA paper that "Communists" are not entitled to equal protection under the law and are not entitled under the First Amendment to have a private political association.

That basic constitutional issue is the axis of the SWP case. Does the First Amendment protect free speech and free political association of everyone, *including* Marxists and others who engage in legal political activity to oppose administration policy?

Civil libertarians say yes. The FBI and its defenders say no.

The bureau is trying hard to recover from months of damaging public scrutiny and criticism. One of the FBI operations most criticized is its ongoing "investigation" of the SWP. Critics of the bureau say that (1) the investigation has been going on for over thirty years without discovering any violent or illegal activity by the party, and (2) FBI officials themselves have admitted *publicly* (including to a House committee) that the party doesn't advocate violence, and never has.

How does the FBI try to defend its actions against the SWP? By arguing that the SWP's Marxist *ideas* mean that the party is likely to engage in violence in the future. The bureau's position is worth quoting at length. The policy is an open and dangerous violation of the First Amendment. Seldom has the bureau been so candid in defending itself.

FBI Director Kelley wrote in a memo dated February 5, 1976, that "the doctrines and objectives of Marxist-Leninist revolutionary organizations and similar groups have provided a basis for the conduct of intelligence investigations concerning them predicated upon the reasonable belief that the government has a legitimate interest in collecting information to assess the extent to which such organizations may contribute to future crises which affect its ability to function." Kelly made clear that the FBI should be able to target groups "even though their objective is not necessarily expressed, or likely to be expressed, in imminent violent action."

Peter Camejo, the SWP's 1976 presidential candidate, called this the "ripe theory" during hearings of the House Intelligence Committee: "That is, that although we do not do so now, at some later date when things are ripe—you might call it the "rotten-ripe theory'—we will turn rotten and then engage in illegal acts and violence. They know very well that our goal is to try to win the majority of the American people to establish some basic change. That is what the Declaration of Independence says we have a right to do.

"The American people have the right to alter the Government, the economy or anything else they want to do. . . . we do not intend to use violence or carry out illegal activities. All we state is that the majority has a right to carry out its activities. That is what we mean by revolution—the right of the American people to make basic changes, as we did in 1776 and as we did in 1861. . . .

"Now, I do believe that this ripe theory, however, *does* apply to the FBI. When they found it ripe, they *did* engage in illegal activities, and when they see the moment is ripe, they are willing to carry out illegal acts."

The logic of the FBI's "ripe theory," of course, is that the FBI can and will label as "potentially rotten" any group who has ideas it doesn't like.

Another side of the government's defense for its assault on the SWP is the FBI's slanderous assertion that the party supports "international terrorism." Also, the FBI charges that the SWP is illegally affiliated with the Fourth International, an international socialist organization that the SWP helped found.

The facts just don't support the FBI's charges. The House

Select Committee on Intelligence reviewed the evidence and found nothing illegal in the SWP's domestic activities or in its solidarity with socialists in other countries.

The FBI's charges have been parroted by a member of Congress who is also a member of the John Birch Society, Rep. Larry McDonald, Democrat of Georgia. The charges also appeared in secret testimony recently published by the Senate Internal Security Subcommittee. The testimony came from a man who represents a public relations outfit known as The Friends of the FBI and who spent the past twenty-five years working for the discredited and extinct House Unamerican Activities Committee and the House Internal Security Committee.

These self-described experts say their information comes from their own research, but it has all the earmarks of FBI intelligence.

What Has Been Accomplished

What are the gains of the suit to date? In the first place, there is no reason to think that much of the information about FBI and CIA illegal activity that has been made public so far would ever have seen the light of day without the initiative of the suit. For example, CIA files released through the suit show the agency has spied on the SWP since 1950, while the official Rockefeller commission report said CIA domestic surveillance began only in the late sixties. Other CIA files, won in the suit, show the agency continues to spy on American citizens.

These revelations have helped educate the American people about the antidemocratic way the employing class maintains its rule. The resulting public outrage has helped put the FBI and the CIA on the defensive. Exposure of their operations, and potential exposure, in the current political climate makes the dirty work of these agencies much harder.

The socialist legal action has helped push Cointelpro to the center of the debate around the FBI. Under this pressure top government officials today insist that Cointelpro is over and done with. They say J. Edgar Hoover ended it on April 28, 1971, only days after news reports of a break-in at the FBI's office in Media, Pennsylvania, shattered the secrecy surrounding the operation.

All available evidence argues convincingly that Cointelpro-style disruption and harassment continue.

Even the FBI memos that ostensibly discontinued Cointelpro are unmistakably worded to allow the agency to engage in future disruption. (These files are reprinted in the introduction to this book.)

Evidence in the socialists' suit includes scores of post-1971 Cointelpro-style incidents. This evidence indicates that the FBI got socialists fired from their jobs and thrown out of their apartments, tried to disrupt their personal lives, and attempted to pressure them into being informers.

The purpose of the suit is to defend the democratic rights of socialists and all working people. Already the exposures of these illegal actions and the response from the public have begun to do that.

Cointelpro itself, massive as it is, is only part of the FBI's secret war on the SWP and the YSA and on others trying to change society. There are indications that the FBI undertook disruption actions before 1956 when Cointelpro began. Even during its so-called Cointelpro years the agency engaged in similar actions outside of that program and instead called them "investigative activity" or "racial matter" or "subversive matter."

For one thing, the FBI's massive burglary operations were not called "Cointelpro." But, like Cointelpro techniques, burglaries continue. The Political Rights Defense Fund has evidence that, at a minimum, the bureau continues to collaborate with right-wing groups and local police to steal information about legal political activities. While FBI Director Kelley asserts that burglaries have ended, he defends their use by saying, "I do not note in these activities any gross abuse of authority. I do not feel that it was a corruption of the trust that was placed in us."

The files that have come out are still rigidly censored. And no one knows for sure how many files remain locked in FBI vaults. The FBI maintains a right to keep secret any information that the bureau says might blow the cover of informers or "investigative methods."

There is far more to the story that what the FBI has been forced to admit thus far. The government hasn't stopped the FBI's abuses. But legal actions by FBI victims such as the Socialist Workers party, the Young Socialist Alliance, and others continue. Those are the main challenge today in the United States to the FBI's unconstitutional activities. Thanks to those efforts we can expect more progress in the battle to get out the full story and put a stop to the FBI's crimes.

SAC NEW YORK June 3, 1960

PERSONAL FOLDER SAC

SOCIALIST WORKERS PARTY-NATIONAL

SOCIALIST WORKERS PARTY - NY LOCAL

On 6/3/60, captioned sources were contacted and made available material maintained in the National and New York Local offices of the SWP, 116 University Place, NYC. Among the items of information obtained from the sources were the following:

(1) Letter dated 6/1/60 setting forth the topic of speech to be given by ~~████████~~, SWP Vice-Presidential-candidate at opening of tour at Detroit, and listing complete schedule of cities to be visited thereafter in nation-wide tour.

(2) Application for membership forms filled out by two individuals and submitted to the SWP (dated in May, 1960)

(3) Letter from individual overseas with an Army signal battalion requesting information about the SWP.

(4) Letter setting forth the new employment of a NYO SI subject

(5) Letter to Canadian Trotskyite setting forth that ~~████████~~ SWP leader would be a speaker for them; giving flight number and time of trip and location of his stay in Toronto.

(6) Letter giving identity of individual subpoenaed to appear before committee (presumably HCUA) in Washington in June and arrangements made by SWP to have American Civil Liberties Union represent this and another individual SWP member subpoenaed.

Pages 204–211: The word "burglary" never appears in the FBI's burglary files. Instead, when the bureau refers to its burglaries, it uses words like "captioned sources" or "highly confidential sources who have access" to the SWP offices. The term "highly confidential sources" has been used in other bureau files in reference to wiretaps. Page 204: An FBI burglary report from 1960 shows that during this entry, bureau agents actually removed files, rather than photographing them. Item six shows the agents stole an SWP letter to the ACLU about the defense of a party member subpoenaed by the House Unamerican Activities Committee.

Memorandum

TO : SAC, NEW YORK   DATE: 7/11/60

FROM : ⟨redacted⟩   PERSONAL ATTENTION—SAC

SUBJECT: SOCIALIST WORKERS PARTY – NATIONAL
⟨redacted⟩

SOCIALIST WORKERS PARTY – NEW YORK LOCAL
⟨redacted⟩

    On 7/11/60, contact was made with ⟨redacted⟩, who have access to material located in national headquarters of the SWP, and with ⟨redacted⟩ who has access to material located in the office of the New York Local, SWP, both at 116 University Place, New York City.

    Approximately 85 photographs were obtained, including such items as the following:

    1) Correspondence identifying contributors to SWP election campaign fund.

    2) Letter establishing trip to be made by SWP leader FARRELL DOBBS.

    3) SWP national financial report of June, 1960.

    4) Breakdown of SWP office expenses of June, 1960.

    5) Letters dated in June and July from ⟨redacted⟩ National Chairman, establishing SWP policy.

    6) SWP Political Committee minutes of June 21 and June 29, 1960.

    7) SWP Resident National Committee minutes of 7/5/60.

    8) Letter of 6/29/60, giving subscriptions obtained in current campaign of "The Militant."

Page 205: Item one in this burglary report shows that the bureau stole names of people who contributed to an SWP election campaign.

SUBJECT: YOUNG SOCIALIST ALLIANCE
         IS - SWP
         ~~████████████~~

I. BACKGROUND

The YOUNG SOCIALIST ALLIANCE (YSA) is the youth organization of the SWP. The SWP utilizes the YSA to further its aims and goals and the YSA is considered, in addition to the action group of the SWP, as the main source of recruits into the Party. The leadership of the YSA on a national basis in NYC and throughout the U.S. on various local bases is composed of SWP members.

II. SECURITY ASPECTS

The National Headquarters, together with the NY Headquarters, and the office of the publication, "Young Socialist," are currently located at 125 Fourth Avenue, NYC. This building is a three-story edifice approximately 25 feet wide by 75 feet in depth. The second and third floors are loft premises. The first floor is occupied by the Sol Karkin Paint Company, Incorporated. The entrance to the second and third floors of the building is a door located beside the paint store. This door leads directly to stair flights to the second and third floors and is secured with a cylinder lock. This entrance does not connect with the paint store on the street level.

~~████████~~ is the owner of the premises, and the owner and operator of the paint store on the street level. NYO indices are negative regarding ~~████~~

The third floor loft of this building is occupied by an artist, ~~████████~~, who maintains a studio. This ...

~~████████~~

Pages 206–208: A "casing" report in which agents carefully describe the offices, with particular attention to placement of street lights, types of locks, and nocturnal habits of neighboring businessmen and residents. These "casing" re-

—individual pursues his profession, together with holding
occasional art classes, in this loft. This activity
transpires' during the daytime. ⟨___⟩ does not reside on
these premises and is not known to frequent the premises
in the evening hours.

        The YSA Headquarters are located on the second
floor loft space. The YSA moved into these headquarters
on 9/21/62. Numerous spot checks of the area have shown
very limited pedestrian and automobile traffic after
midnight. The buildings adjacent to this location
between 12th and 13th Streets, on both sides of the street,
are commercial establishments and lofts, and contain
no residence.

        It has been ascertained that the paint store
at this building closes at 6:00 p.m. and that all of the
commercial establishments in this area close business
between 5:00 and 6:00 p.m.

        Entrance will be made between the hours of
twelve midnight and 4:00 a.m., on 9/28/62.

        Security will be assured prior to entry on
this assignment.

ports show also that one of the FBI's purposes in the burglaries was to collect the names of all members. Other
burglary files show the bureau used burglaries to gather
information to use in Cointelpro disruption operations.

III. PURPOSE OF ASSIGNMENT

To locate the national and local records relating to the YSA, together with the identity of the national officers and members. It is also anticipated that numerous records of both the local organization and YSA branches throughout the country will be made available.

IV. PERSONNEL

████████████████████████ and █████████████ are responsible for the survey and establishment of the source.

████████████████████ will be on the scene and responsible for the assignment. The following agents will participate in the assignment:

████████ ████████

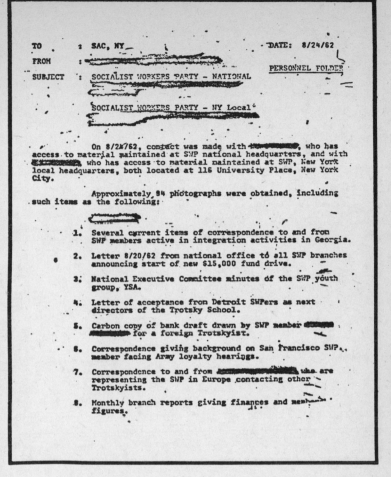

TO : SAC, NY___   DATE: 8/24/62
FROM :
                                                   PERSONNEL FOLDER
SUBJECT : SOCIALIST WORKERS PARTY - NATIONAL

        SOCIALIST WORKERS PARTY - NY Local

        On 8/24/62, contact was made with ███████, who has
access to material maintained at SWP national headquarters, and with
███████, who has access to material maintained at SWP, New York
local headquarters, both located at 116 University Place, New York
City.

        Approximately 94 photographs were obtained, including
such items as the following:

    1. Several current items of correspondence to and from
       SWP members active in integration activities in Georgia.

    2. Letter 8/20/62 from national office to all SWP branches
       announcing start of new $15,000 fund drive.

    3. National Executive Committee minutes of the SWP youth
       group, YSA.

    4. Letter of acceptance from Detroit SWPers as next
       directors of the Trotsky School.

    5. Carbon copy of bank draft drawn by SWP member ███████
       ███████ for a foreign Trotskyist.

    6. Correspondence giving background on San Francisco SWP
       member facing Army loyalty hearings.

    7. Correspondence to and from ███████ who are
       representing the SWP in Europe contacting other
       Trotskyists.

    8. Monthly branch reports giving finances and member
       figures.

*Page 209: Item six in this burglary report shows the bureau
took correspondence about a defense case of a party member. Item one shows spying on SWP members "active in
integration activities in Georgia."*

1. NYL, SWP Executive Committee minutes for May, June, 1963.

2. Information re arrangements for SWP National Convention.

3. Financial Data of NYL, SWP, June, 1963.

4. Correspondence re out-of-town subjects attending SWP convention.

5. Address of Detroit subjects living in NYC.

6. Identity of unsub foreign trotskyist.

It should be noted that it was necessary on this occasion to pick the lock on the street entrance of the building in order to get inside. This was accomplished by ~~~~~~ Jr., who also made a new key for the front door.

PERSONNEL PARTICIPATING

Page 210: *The agents who did the burglaries used keys. This report, dated June 28, 1963 (the second page of which is reprinted here), notes that it was necessary to pick a lock that had been changed and that a new key was made on the spot.*

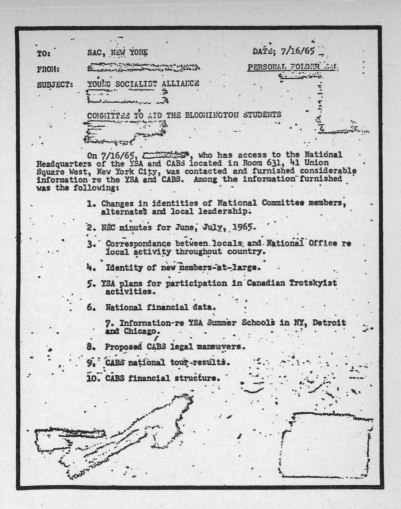

COMMITTEE TO AID THE BLOOMINGTON STUDENTS

On 7/16/65, ~~~~~~~, who has access to the National Headquarters of the YSA and CABS located in Room 631, 41 Union Square West, New York City, was contacted and furnished considerable information re the YSA and CABS. Among the information furnished was the following:

1. Changes in identities of National Committee members, alternates and local leadership.

2. NEC minutes for June, July, 1965.

3. Correspondance between locals and National Office re local activity throughout country.

4. Identity of new members-at-large.

5. YSA plans for participation in Canadian Trotskyist activities.

6. National financial data.

7. Information re YSA Summer Schools in NY, Detroit and Chicago.

8. Proposed CABS legal maneuvers.

9. CABS national tour results.

10. CABS financial structure.

Page 211: Item eight in this burglary report shows the bureau stole information about legal strategy in the defense of three YSA members who were students at the University of Indiana at Bloomington. The students were charged with "conspiring to overthrow the State of Indiana." The Committee to Aid the Bloomington Students (CABS) was set up to support and finance their defense. Bertrand Russell was the honorary chairman of the committee and Leonard Boudin was chief counsel for the students.

Notes

1. Henry Steele Commager, "The Constitution Is Alive and Well," *New York Times*, August 11, 1974. Commager, who has been forceful in defense of civil liberties and opposition to the Indochina war, states that prior to Nixon, "no President has ever attempted to subvert" the Constitution or "challenged the basic assumptions of our constitutional system itself." But "the system worked" and the challenge was defeated.

2. Press release of the Department of Justice, released by Attorney General William B. Saxbe and FBI Director Clarence M. Kelley, November 18, 1974.

3. See *New York Times*, August 4, 1974, for documents and commentary.

4. John M. Crewdson, "Levi Reveals More Harassment by F.B.I.," *New York Times*, May 24, 1975. Also, Associated Press, *Boston Globe*, May 24, 1975.

5. Memorandum of July 1, 1968. This is not the only example of FBI efforts to interfere in academic affairs. Attorney General Edward Levi testified before the Senate Select Committee on Intelligence that "he had once been a recipient of a counterintelligence letter aimed at discrediting a professor at the university" (he was then president). The anonymous letter was sent by the FBI to the board of trustees and the press concerning the antiwar activities of Richard Flacks, "who was later beaten by an unidentified assailant for his political views," a few months after "members of a radical right-wing group called the Legion of Justice had attacked students . . ." (*New York Times*, December 19, 1975). The letter was sent in the hope that "it may discourage Flacks or even result in his ultimate removal from the University of Chicago" (FBI memorandum, August 2, 1968), but without discernible results, the bureau reported. In another case, "the FBI approved furnishing information to a responsible Harvard University official that a student who was employed by the University was involved in Students for a Democratic Society (SDS) activities. Shortly thereafter, the student lost his job" (report of the House

Select Committee on Intelligence, citing a Cointelpro memorandum, *Village Voice* supplement, February 16, 1976; henceforth, Pike Committee Report). See also note 6 below.

6. On the latter, see Vin McLellan, "FBI Heists Names of 1970 Student Strikers," *Boston Phoenix,* March 5, 1974, based on the report of former security officers at Brandeis University.

7. John M. Crewdson, "Black Pastor Got F.B.I. Threat in '69," *New York Times,* March 17, 1975.

8. Nicholas M. Horrock, *New York Times,* November 19 and 20, 1975; Robert Adams and Martha Shirk, *St. Louis Post-Dispatch,* November 19, 1975.

9. Harry Kelly, "FBI spurred gang fight in Chicago, Senate says," *Chicago Tribune,* November 20, 1975. The head of the FBI Chicago field office at the time that the letter was sent testified in federal court that its purpose was entirely nonviolent, and that it would not have been approved "if it had referred to violence of any kind" (Rob Warden, *Chicago Daily News,* February 11, 1976).

10. For a review of some of these actions, see Dave Dellinger, *More Power than We Know* (New York: Doubleday, 1975); Gary T. Marx, "Thoughts on a Neglected Category of Social Movement Participant: The Agent Provocateur and the Informant," *American Journal of Sociology,* vol. 80, no. 2 (September 1974), pp. 402-42.

11. Mike Royko, *Chicago Daily News; Boston Globe,* February 1, 1975. Royko's source refused to take his information to the investigating agencies, on the grounds that "these local prosecutors . . . were involved in the same kind of thing" and will "wind up looking at themselves in a mirror."

12. For information on these and other FBI actions in Seattle, see Dellinger, *op. cit.,* and Frank J. Donner, "Hoover's Legacy," *The Nation,* June 1, 1974.

13. John M. Crewdson, "Ex-Operative Says He Worked for F.B.I. To Disrupt Political Activities Up To '74," *New York Times,* February 24, 1975.

14. *Civil Liberties,* No. 273, December 1970; publication of the ACLU.

15. Dellinger, *op. cit.*

16. John Kifner, "F.B.I. Gave Chicago Police Plan of Slain Panther's Apartment," *New York Times,* May 25, 1974. Although the fact of FBI involvement in the Hampton assassination, along with other details of this major state crime, was not widely publicized outside of Chicago, nevertheless there were a few reports, such as this one. There can be no excuse for the general silence on this matter, which alone overshadows the entire Watergate affair by a substantial margin.

17. John Kifner, "Security Aide for Indians Says He Was F.B.I. Informer," *New York Times,* March 13, 1975.

18. *Special Report of Interagency Committee on Intelligence* (Ad Hoc), Chairman, J. Edgar Hoover, along with the directors of the CIA, DIA, and NSA, prepared for the President, June 25, 1970, marked "Top Secret."

A censored version was later released. Quotes below are from Book 7, Part 1: *Summary of Internal Security Threat.*

19. Everett R. Holles, "A.C.L.U. Says F.B.I. Funded 'Army' To Terrorize Antiwar Protesters," *New York Times,* June 27, 1975. Information and quotes given below are from the eighteen-page single-spaced report submitted to the Senate Select Committee on June 27, 1975, unless otherwise indicated. See also Steven V. Roberts, "F.B.I. Informer Is Linked to Right-Wing Violence," *New York Times,* June 24, 1974.

20. Godfrey "has testified in a California court that the bureau gave him $10,000 to $20,000 worth of weapons and explosives for use by the [SAO] in addition to his $250-a-month salary as an informant." John M. Crewdson, "Kelley Discounts F.B.I.'s Link to a Terrorist Group," *New York Times,* January 12, 1976.

21. The report also notes that FBI agents and Cambridge, Massachusetts, police broke into the apartment of George Katsiaficas, "ransacked it and stole his personal diaries and other papers and effects," according to court testimony at a criminal trial by the Cambridge police officer involved. Katsiaficas and Bohmer were friends in Cambridge and involved in common political activities there. Both went to San Diego. Both were targeted by the SAO and are currently plaintiffs in a civil suit supported by the ACLU in San Diego.

22. I have discussed another clear-cut example in *Problems of Knowledge and Freedom* (Pantheon, 1971), p. 72. There are many others. To my knowledge, there has been no systematic investigation of this matter.

23. "F.B.I. Chief Tells of Coast Informant," *New York Times,* January 14, 1976, p. 57. Reporting Kelley's denials, here and on January 12 (see note 20), the *Times* also cited some of the charges, attributing them to the discoveries of Senate Committee investigators, though the information cited was contained in the June 1975 ACLU report, as the *Times* itself reported at the time (see note 19).

24. Everett R. Holles, "San Diego Seeking Inquiry Into F.B.I.," *New York Times,* February 8, 1976. Holles also refers to "evidence assembled by the Senate committee's investigators," citing information in the June 1975 ACLU report that appeared in the *Times* that month. The *Times* reports in January and February, 1976, suggest that a Senate inquiry into the matter is in progress but give no evidence that this is so. The February 2 resolution of the San Diego City Council indicates that there has been no serious investigation. The question will be settled by the Church Committee report.

25. For analysis and texts of the Media documents, see Paul Cowan, Nick Egleson, and Nat Hentoff, *State Secrets* (Holt, Rinehart and Winston, 1973). Comparable figures are given by Marx (*op. cit.*). He notes that "among the 34 cases [of infiltration] for which some information is available, 11 involved white campus groups; 11, predominantly white peace groups and/or economic groups; 10, black and Chicano groups; and only two, right-wing groups." Furthermore, "in two-thirds of the 34 cases considered here, the specious activists appear to have gone beyond pas-

sive information gathering to active provocation." It had been speculated that Cointelpro was terminated (officially at least) after the program was exposed by the Media burglary. This is confirmed in a briefing with the Assistant Director of the FBI in charge of the Intelligence Division. (See Pike Committee Report.)

26. C. Gerald Fraser, "F.B.I. Action in 1961 Called Still Harmful to Hopes of Blacks," *New York Times,* April 6, 1974. See also Jesse Jackson and Alvin F. Poussaint, "The Danger Behind FBI Obstruction of Black Movements," *Boston Globe,* April 2, 1974.

27. "Charges Over F.B.I.'s Tactics on Subversive Suspects Barred," *Washington Star-News; New York Times,* January 4, 1975.

28. The Committee Report notes that the FBI Manual of Instructions allows preliminary investigations of "extremist" groups, but requires that these be terminated in ninety days if there is no indication of criminal violations.

29. Letter to the annual Chief Justice Earl Warren Conference on Advocacy, June 7-8, 1974, cited from the final report, *Privacy in a Free Society,* by Nat Hentoff, "The Privacy War Games," *The Village Voice,* December 9, 1974.

30. Frank Wilkinson, *The Era of Libertarian Repression—1948 to 1973: from Congressman to President, with Substantial Support from the Liberal Establishment,* University of Akron, 1974; reprinted from the *University of Akron Law Review.*

31. Emergency Detention Act of 1950, cited by Wilkinson.

32. Cited by Wilkinson from *96 Congressional Record,* 1950, 15520-1.

33. See my *For Reasons of State* (Pantheon, 1973) and earlier books. Also my "Reporting Indochina: the News Media and the Legitimation of Lies," *Social Policy,* October 1973; "The Remaking of History," *Ramparts,* August 1975. See also (with E.S. Herman) *Counterrevolutionary Violence: Bloodbaths in Fact and Propaganda* (Warner Modular, 1973), suppressed by order of the parent conglomerate (Warner Brothers) but available in French (*Bains de Sang,* Seghers/Laffont, 1974) and other European languages. It should be noted that there was a fair amount of honest and important work by foreign correspondents in the field, and occasional instances of accurate and serious review and analysis at the editorial level as well. For an outstanding example, see the review of the war in the special supplement of the *St. Louis Post-Dispatch* under the direction of Richard Dudman, April 30, 1975.

34. On the post-World War I "Red Scare" see Murray B. Levin, *Political Hysteria in America: The Democratic Capacity for Repression* (Basic Books, 1971). Other sources have cited figures as high as 10,000 arrested during the Palmer Raids and 700 aliens deported. See Max Lowenthal, *The Federal Bureau of Investigation* (William Sloane Associates, Inc., 1950.)

35. David Brion Davis, editor, *The Fear of Conspiracy* (Cornell University Press, 1971).

36. *Ibid.* A fifth committed suicide before the sentence of death could be

executed. Three others were sentenced to hanging as well, but were not executed. No proof was offered that any of the eight had been involved in the bomb-throwing.

37. See the excerpt from Michael J. Schaack, *Anarchy and Anarchists,* Chicago, 1889, in Davis's collection. Schaack was captain of the East Chicago Avenue Police Station and "was widely credited with having uncovered the anarchist conspiracy" (Davis).

38. See excerpts from Palmer in Davis, *op cit.* On the role of the press, see Levin, *op cit.*

39. Cited by Levin.

40. See except in Davis, *op. cit.*

41. Cf. Levin, *op. cit.*

42. Foster Rhea Dulles, *The Road to Teheran* (Princeton, 1945), cited by Levin, *op. cit.*

43. See the concurring and dissenting opinions of Mr. Justice Jackson cited in Davis, *op. cit.*

44. Nicholas M. Horrock, "The F.B.I.'s Appetite for Very Small Potatoes," *New York Times,* March 23, 1975.

45. On the significance of the threat, both actual and potential, as perceived at high levels of policy planning, see my review of some of the evidence contained in the "Pentagon Papers" in *For Reasons of State,* chapter 1. For discussion of the impact on the American expeditionary force, see David Cortright, *Soldiers in Revolt,* (New York, Doubleday, 1975).

NELSON BLACKSTOCK is an editor of *The Militant,* a socialist newsweekly, and a member of the Socialist Workers Party National Committee.

Mr. Blackstock was born in Savannah, Georgia, on September 7, 1944. His political activity began in the early sixties, when he was among the few white Southerners to become active in the civil rights movement. In 1964 he joined the staff of the Student Nonviolent Coordinating Committee (SNCC) and took part in its Mississippi Freedom Summer. That same year he was a founder of the Southern Student Organizing Commiteee (SSOC).

In Atlanta during 1965 and 1966 Mr. Blackstock helped organize some of the first antiwar demonstrations in the South. In 1967 he and others formed a chapter of the Young Socialist Alliance in Atlanta. Recently released FBI files revealed that as a result of his socialist and antiwar activity, Mr. Blackstock himself was pinpointed for two separate Cointelpro operations in Atlanta in the late sixties.

Mr. Blackstock was the National Organizational Secretary of the Young Socialist Alliance in 1969-70.

While living in Houston in the early seventies, Mr. Blackstock served as Texas state chairman of the Socialist Workers party.

He has also been the editor of the *Young Socialist* magazine and an associate editor of the *International Socialist Review.*

Mr. Blackstock lives in Hoboken, New Jersey.

PROFESSOR NOAM CHOMSKY, an eminent and revolutionary scholar in the field of linguistics, has in recent years become a figure of national attention through his brilliant criticism of American political life. He received his B.A., M.A., and Ph.D. from the University of Pennsylvania and was a Fellow at Harvard from 1951 to 1955. In 1955 he was appointed to the faculty of the Massachusetts Institute of Technology, and in 1961 he became a full professor. In addition he has served as a visiting professor at the University of California, Los Angeles, and at Berkeley, and as a Research Fellow at the Institute for Advanced Study at Princeton and the Center for Cognitive Studies at Harvard.

Among his many books and articles on linguistics, philosophy, intellectual history and contemporary issues are *American Power and the New Mandarins, Problems of Knowledge and Freedom, For Reasons of State* and *Peace in the Middle East?*